THE DESCENT OF
JAPANESE FATHER GOD

AME
NO
MIOYA
GAMI

HS PRESS

THE DESCENT OF
JAPANESE FATHER GOD

AME
NO
MIOYA
GAMI

天御祖神

THE "GOD OF CREATION" IN
THE ANCIENT DOCUMENT *HOTSUMA TSUTAE*

RYUHO OKAWA

HS PRESS

HS Press is an imprint of IRH Press Co., Ltd.
Tokyo
ISBN 13: 978-1-943928-35-4
ISBN 10: 1-943928-35-5
Cover Image: vchal/Shutterstock.com
Shun Tokiya/Shutterstock.com
Interior Image: A⊕ineko/PIXTA
be hiro/PIXTA
JIJI
Second Edition

Contents

PART TWO

The Lecture on *The Descent of Ame-no-Mioya-Gami*

CHAPTER ONE

The Lecture on *The Descent of Ame-no-Mioya-Gami*
The Origin of the Japanese Civilization

Q&A Session

Exploring Deeper into the Secrets of Japan and the Universe

Afterword 251

PART ONE

The Descent of Japanese Father God Ame-no-Mioya-Gami

The "God of Creation"
in the ancient document
Hotsuma Tsutae

These spiritual messages were channeled through Ryuho Okawa. However, please note that because of his high level of enlightenment, his way of receiving spiritual messages is fundamentally different from other psychic mediums who undergo trances and are completely taken over by the spirits they are channeling.

It should be noted that these spiritual messages are opinions of the individual spirits and may contradict the ideas or teachings of Happy Science Group.

Preface

You will probably find it a very mysterious book.

This book—my 2500th publication—might be the modern *Hotsuma Tsutae.* It teaches Japanese people that Japan's civilized history is not about 3,000 years long but 30,000 years. And, it also teaches that it was Japanese civilization that was passed down to the Eurasian continent and the Mu continent, contrary to the commonly accepted knowledge of today.

Most importantly, it tells that the God of Creation that should be described in the Japanese myths is the Messiah called "Ame-no-Mioya-Gami," who had come from the Andromeda Galaxy. This is the first book in the world that describes how he had descended from the sky.

Ame-no-Mioya-Gami is a spiritual being who is still shrouded in much mystery, but first, for now, I hope you can withstand this impact on your knowledge.

Ryuho Okawa
Master & CEO of Happy Science Group
January 13, 2019

CHAPTER ONE

Who Is Ame-no-Mioya-Gami?

Originally recorded in Japanese on October 3, 2015
at General Headquarters, Happy Science, Japan
and later translated into English.

Ame-no-Mioya-Gami

The Father God who appears in the ancient document, *Hotsuma Tsutae*, which is said to be older than *Kojiki* (Records of Ancient Matters) and *Nihon Shoki* (Chronicles of Japan). According to Happy Science spiritual research, He is the same spiritual Being as Lord God, whom Jesus called "Father."

In this chapter, there are a total of three interviewers from Happy Science, symbolized as A, B, and C in the order that they first appear.

1

Unlocking the Secrets of Japanese Father God Ame-no-Mioya-Gami

There are very few documentary records about Ame-no-Mioya-Gami

RYUHO OKAWA

Today (October 3, 2015), I would like to examine Ame-no-Mioya-Gami, although it may be too late in a sense. I have a piece of paper here given for my reference. I took a look at it, wondering where the material came from and found it was all excerpts from my own books. It has three excerpts—one from *Nihon Shinto-teki Kofuku-ron* (literally, "Happiness Theory based on Japanese Shinto") and others from the afterwords of *Shin no Heiwa ni Mukete* (literally, "Toward True Peace") and *The Truth about WWII: Justice Pal Speaks on the Tokyo Trials* (Tokyo: HS Press, 2015). I feel there's not much point in referring to my own writings, but this means there is no other material on Ame-no-Mioya-Gami. I am not even sure whether his name is pronounced Ame-no-Mioya-Kami, Ame-no-Mioya-no-Kami, or Ame-no-Mioya-Gami. It is unclear because there is no shrine related to him or no place worshiping him.

As far as I know, his name appears in a historical document called *Hotsuma Tsutae*, but it may also appear in other documents. *Hotsuma Tsutae* itself is not recognized as an official historical record in Japanese history. I'm not sure if it really is one of the original historical documents that existed prior to *Kojiki* and *Nihon Shoki*. Another theory suggests it was written in the medieval period of Japan or during the Edo period (1603–1868). But *Hotsuma Tsutae* is written in the unique ancient Japanese characters called *hotsuma* characters.

Cuneiform characters used in Mesopotamia civilization.

Hotsuma characters that are said to have been used in ancient Japan before kanji characters were introduced.

Hieroglyphs used in ancient Egypt.

They are similar to the so-called cuneiform letters—ancient characters used in the areas around Iraq—and the hieroglyphs used in Egypt. The shape of these characters makes me think they share the same root. Suppose there truly was someone who invented hotsuma characters in the medieval period. In that case, that person must be as talented as those who created constructed languages such as Latin and Sanskrit.

In any case, it is true that the further you go back in time, the more obscure Japanese history becomes. There is also a strong tendency to trace history archeologically. However, from an archeological dig, you can only find things like shell mounds, earthenware, bronze mirrors, or bronze swords, and it is quite difficult to find proof that there was an advanced civilization or faith in ancient times. So we are not sure about the era more ancient than the times described in *Kojiki* and *Nihon Shoki*. It may be like the primitive times when people practiced crouched burials and placed a big stone on the burial ground. It is difficult to know.

Hotsuma Tsutae describes the first god differently from Kojiki and Nihon Shoki

RYUHO OKAWA

Kojiki, which is believed to have been compiled in AD 712, is a history book written in the Japanese language (a variant of classical Chinese), and it has many mythological aspects. On the other hand, *Nihon Shoki* is believed to have been compiled in about AD 720, and is all written in classical Chinese. This is most likely because it was written to show Japanese history to foreign countries, or mainly to China. A lot of mythological aspects are omitted from this *Nihon Shoki*.

1) The first god that appears in *Kojiki*

To explain in more detail, the first god that appears in *Kojiki* is Ame-no-Minakanushi-no-Kami. He is described as the god at the center of heaven or the universe. He is a *hitori-gami*, meaning god who does not marry, and he appears like a god of the sky who has no physical body.

2) The first god that appears in *Nihon Shoki*

On the other hand, in *Nihon Shoki*, which was compiled just eight years after *Kojiki* was written, the gods that appear at the beginning of *Kojiki* are all removed. Instead, Kuni-no-Tokotachi-no-Kami—who appears later in *Kojiki*—appears first and is described as the first god.

3) The first god that appears in *Hotsuma Tsutae*

Hotsuma Tsutae is written in the ancient characters (hotsuma characters). It seems that they can be read by applying the Japanese syllabary. I do not know why it is possible, but researchers have managed to read them. It may be the same as reading ancient hieroglyphs. I do feel that hotsuma characters are different from the Japanese letters, but it seems that there was a writing system in Japan that was different from the one used in China or the Korean Peninsula.

This *Hotsuma Tsutae* has a different view from *Kojiki* and *Nihon Shoki*. It describes Ame-no-Mioya-Gami as the first god, followed by Ame-no-Minakanushi-no-Kami as the second god, and then Kuni-no-Tokotachi-no-Kami as the third god. Three gods appear in this order. This is the only material I have ever seen that mentions the name Ame-no-Mioya-Gami.

What is more, from what I have read, Kuni-no-Tokotachi-no-Kami was the first emperor of Japan, so he was born with a physical body. There is also a description that upon returning to heaven, he became Ame-no-Minakanushi-no-Kami. There seems to be some contradiction in these descriptions.

How should we interpret the description that Amaterasu-O-Mikami was a male god?

RYUHO OKAWA

A theory states that Amaterasu-O-Mikami (see p.105) was a male god, and *Hotsuma Tsutae* strongly takes this stance. The name Amaterasu-O-Mikami is mentioned many times in *Hotsuma Tsutae*. It doesn't appear so much in *Kojiki* and *Nihon Shoki*, but it repeatedly appears in *Hotsuma Tsutae*. *Hotsuma Tsutae* describes that when Amaterasu-O-Mikami was ruling this world, Amaterasu received guidance from Ame-no-Mioya-Gami, who was in heaven. But according to *Kojiki*, Amaterasu was in heaven when the grandson Ninigi-no-Mikoto descended on Mt. Takachiho-no-Mine and became the ancestor of the imperial family. And it says that Ninigi-no-Mikoto and the generations after that had a physical body.

So, *Hotsuma Tsutae* describes that Amaterasu-O-Mikami appeared on the earth. What is more, it says that Amaterasu was a male god and had wives. The wives' names are also written as well as the descriptions about the children. I am not sure why there are such descriptions.

The imperial throne is succeeded by male-line males in the later ages, and Amaterasu-O-Mikami is believed to be the physical ancestor of the imperial family. This has been the case since the pre-World War II period. But from what I've read in *Kojiki*, Amaterasu-O-Mikami is not described as the physical ancestor of the imperial family but as a god in heaven, and it was the grandson Ninigi-no-Mikoto and the generations after him that were manifested into physical bodies. From its writing, we can't necessarily say that Amaterasu-O-Mikami is the physical ancestor of the imperial family.

Suppose Amaterasu-O-Mikami had truly lived on the earth and had wives and children, as *Hotsuma Tsutae* describes. In that case, this certainly means Amaterasu came down to this world with a physical body. What is more, if Amaterasu-O-Mikami were truly male, it would mean that the emperors are the descendants of a male god Amaterasu and it would make sense that the lineage of the male line was maintained. For this reason, I cannot completely exclude the possibility that *Hotsuma Tsutae* was written in later periods than *Kojiki* and *Nihon Shoki* to justify the rule of the imperial family.

But considering that it was written in ancient characters, it feels strange.

As a side note, both Tsukuyomi-no-Mikoto and Susanoo-no-Mikoto are described as male gods in *Hotsuma Tsutae*, so the Three Deities are all described as male. According to *Kojiki* and *Nihon Shoki*, Izanagi-no-Okami purified himself from the Izanami's curse in Awagihara upon returning from the land of the dead. And when he first washed his left eye, Amaterasu-O-Mikami was born; when he washed his right eye, Tsukuyomi was born; and when he washed his nose, Susanoo was born. These were the Three Deities. About 10 other gods, including some goddesses, were born as he washed his armor and other parts of his body. But since this story has a lot of mythological overtones, it is not clear.

While Amaterasu-O-Mikami is described more like a female god in *Kojiki*, it can be read as a male god in *Nihon Shoki*. Even though the imperial court compiled these two documents respectively in 712 and 720, they contradict each other so much that it is hard to understand the truth. Our spiritual research has revealed that the soul of Amaterasu-O-Mikami contains both male and female spirits, so from a spiritual point of view, she can be considered as both male and female. Therefore, those descriptions were probably not written by investigating the actual gender when Amaterasu was alive on earth. Given that there must have been mediums who could receive messages from gods, Amaterasu was possibly described as either a male god or a female god depending on how Amaterasu appeared when summoned.

In any case, both *Kojiki* and *Nihon Shoki* are said to have been compiled by collecting and sorting out material from *Fudoki* (descriptions of regional culture, products, legends, etc.) that had existed in various regions of Japan. I think some decisions were most likely made on what to include and what to exclude.

There is a theory stating that gods are genderless

RYUHO OKAWA

There is also a theory stating that Empress Jito (645-703) made Amaterasu-O-Mikami a female god to justify her rule. Looking at the mainstream ideas of Japanese Shinto, the imperial family, and shrines of Japan today, Amaterasu-O-Mikami is regarded more like a female god. When I went to Amano Iwato Shrine in Takachiho, I saw a bronze statue of Amaterasu-O-Mikami at the entrance. It was portrayed as a slim woman with an oval face. There are also drawings of Amaterasu coming out of Ama-no-iwato (rock cave) with a brilliant glow, much like the resurrection of Jesus Christ. In these drawings, Amaterasu is depicted as a female god. So, I think there is a strong tendency to regard her as female today.

In addition, there is a moral education book used before and during World War II, which was seemingly based on the Imperial Rescript on Education. It portrays Amaterasu-O-Mikami as a female god. So, I think the female image was already fixed by that time.

Our spiritual research on various people's past lives so far has revealed that people can be born as male or female. So, there is probably no point in delving into the details about gender. Some say that gods are genderless, and the spirits at the level of tathagata and higher are neither male nor female.

A statue of Amaterasu-O-Mikami at Amano Iwato Shrine (in Takachiho, Miyazaki Prefecture).

Others say that high spirits are all neuters. Indeed, there is some truth in such theories. Gods have both paternal and maternal aspects, and gender is just one physical appearance when they have physical bodies on earth. So maybe gods have no gender in the other world.

The descriptions of Ame-no-Mioya-Gami in my other books

RYUHO OKAWA

In *Nihon Shinto-teki Kofuku-ron* ("Happiness Theory based on Japanese Shinto"), I wrote that Ame-no-Minakanushi-no-Kami appears in *Hotsuma Tsutae* as a branch spirit of Ame-no-Mioya-Gami. I also wrote that *Kojiki* has no equivalent story to the Genesis in the Old Testament and *Hotsuma Tsutae* fills in that missing part.

As a side note, the founder of the Japanese religion Tenrikyo, Miki Nakayama—who is said to have been one of the past lives of my mother—wrote *Doroumi Koki* ("Ancient Records of the Muddy Waters"). It describes the super ancient times dating back more than 900 million years. It says the creation of the world started when something like a turtle—not fish—was crawling in the muddy ocean like the Ariake sea. I guess a story that tells about Genesis is necessary for a religion to become a world religion.

And in the afterword of *Shin no Heiwa ni Mukete* ("Toward True Peace") I wrote, "I revealed that I myself had guided historical Jesus Christ from heaven and that I am Lord God whom he called 'Father.' This Heavenly Father is the same spiritual being as Ame-no-Mioya-Gami who existed before Amaterasu-O-Mikami of Japanese Shinto."

In the afterword of *The Truth about WWII: Justice Pal Speaks on the Tokyo Trials*, I boldly wrote, "There is the Original God. He is called Vishnu in the Indian Spirit World and Ame-no-Mioya-Gami in the Japanese Spirit World. He has a lot of lower gods who split off from him in various forms," and "The roots of the Japanese civilization are thought to be in the Mu civilization and the roots of the Indian civilization are thought to be in the Lemuria civilization. Both Mu and Lemuria are thought to have been guided by the same World God."

I did not mention any relationship between Vishnu and El Cantare in *The Laws of the Sun* (New York: IRH Press, 2018). I was probably not fully aware of the connection between them when I wrote *The Laws of the Sun* around the age of 30.

The position of Vishnu may change in the future

RYUHO OKAWA

It's true that in Hinduism today—or Brahmanism in ancient times—in India, Vishnu is considered to have overwhelming power and is regarded like the Primordial God. In India, even Shakyamuni Buddha is understood as one part of Vishnu. Vishnu is portrayed to have many faces, much like the multi-faced Buddha statues, and it is said that Buddha is one of Vishnu's faces. So, Buddhism has been absorbed into Hinduism in present-day India. In this sense, Hinduism does not deny Buddhism but recognizes that Shakyamuni is one of the manifestations of Vishnu in this world.

When I wrote *The Laws of the Sun* in the early days, I recognized Hinduism as one of the ethnic religions, so I did not delve deeply into the subject. Currently, India has a population of 1.3 billion, and it is expected to exceed the population of China soon. India is now growing as a world

Ten avatars of Vishnu.

power, and it is said that India will most likely compete with China for hegemony. So it's possible that Hinduism, which was thought to be an ethnic religion, could develop into becoming a world religion. If this happens, I think Vishnu's position can change into the world-level God.

India's outlook on the universe is similar to what is described in our space people readings

RYUHO OKAWA

There are many descriptions in relation to Vishnu, and one of them goes like this: "This universe, including Earth and the Milky Way Galaxy, is a world that appeared in Vishnu's dream when he was taking a nap on a lotus leaf in heaven." There is such a large-scale story. But similar stories often appear in our space people readings[1] and in my lectures. For example, I have said the following in my lecture: "The universe, which our galaxy belongs to and we are looking at, is like a drop of water floating in the true universe, and there are many such 'drops of water' floating in the universe." I've also said, "The universe that contains our galaxy is equivalent to the right eye of the entire universe." These views themselves are quite close to Vishnu's view of the universe. I don't use manuscripts in my lectures and speak as I receive inspiration, so I sometimes don't know where the messages are coming from. But there could indeed be such an aspect to the universe. So I think there is still room for our understanding to change.

Especially now that our missionary activities in India have gained momentum, I sometimes think it would be convenient to state that Vishnu is the same as El Cantare. It might be better for us to incorporate Vishnu. If you are asked who El Cantare is, you can simply answer: "He is Vishnu." Then it would be easier to understand, so we should probably connect Vishnu to El Cantare. Judaism often talks about the World God, but there are only a little over 10 million Jewish people in the world, and they are quite small compared to India's large population of 1.3 billion people. We probably need to consider this point as well. India is in conflict with Pakistan, but if we say, "Their Allah is the same as Vishnu," we could connect them as well. I'm not sure they will forgive us for saying so, but it's one possibility.

Properly speaking, I should state my views after investigating Ame-no-Mioya-Gami. Since I have already written various things about him before any research, I have gotten a head start.

Summoning the spirit of Ame-no-Mioya-Gami

RYUHO OKAWA

Now, I wonder who will appear when I call this god. In fact, I have never summoned him, so I really don't know who will appear. He might say, "I'm Ra Mu," or "I'm Shakyamuni," or name some other god—I don't know. Or it could end up that no one appears, or a being who calls himself as Ame-no-Mioya-Gami might simply appear.

As I mentioned earlier, in *Hotsuma Tsutae*, Ame-no-Mioya-Gami appears first among other Japanese gods, then Ame-no-Minakanushi-no-Kami, followed by Kuni-Tokotachi-no-Kami. But from what I've checked, I found a curious description that says Ame-no-Mioya-Gami was born on the earth once. What does it mean to be the first god and Primordial God and was also born on the earth? If he was born on the earth previously, he should have been born in Japan or areas connected to Japan. A god who had split from him might have existed in ancient Japan. I don't know anything about this. He might start to say that he was born on earth and founded Japan 10,000 years ago.

Anyway, he is shrouded in mystery, so I'm not sure if he will appear when I summon him. If he appears, who will he identify himself as? God has many faces and names, so it's difficult to understand. I don't know what will happen because I have never directly summoned him before. If he insists on calling himself Ame-no-Mioya-Gami, it would be fine to go along with it. I hope you will ask him various questions and get a general image of him.

These are my introductory remarks. So now, I will summon Ame-no-Mioya-Gami and leave the rest up to you.

A

We understand.

RYUHO OKAWA

Well, I cannot deny the possibility that it will be over in about five minutes.

[*Claps once.*] Then, [*claps once*] I would like to summon Ame-no-Mioya-no-Kami here at Happy Science Headquarters.

O Ame-no-Mioya-Gami [*claps once*], Ame-no-Mioya-no-Kami [*claps once*], please come down to Happy Science General Headquarters [*keeps clapping slowly*] and tell us about your work and guidance as the Original God or Primordial God of Japan, if any.

O Ame-no-Mioya-no-Kami, Ame-no-Mioya-no-Kami, Ame-no-Mioya-Gami, please come down to Happy Science General Headquarters and show us your true identity in relation to Japan.

O Ame-no-Mioya-no-Kami, Ame-no-Mioya-no-Kami, Ame-no-Mioya-Gami...

[About 20 seconds of silence while clapping in a steady rhythm.]

[About 30 seconds of silence.]

2

Ame-no-Mioya-Gami Speaks in Tongues

Asking about Ame-no-Mioya-Gami's relation to the gods of India

A

Are you Lord Ame-no-Mioya-Gami? Thank you very much for coming down to the prayer room of Happy Science General Headquarters today.

AME-NO-MIOYA-GAMI

Hmm... hmm... hmm... hmm... [*Claps twice. About five seconds of silence.*] Hmm...

A

We, the Japanese people, don't know much about Lord Ame-no-Mioya-Gami. Your name appears only in the ancient document called *Hotsuma Tsutae*, which is an unofficial Japanese ancient history book. It gives us just a glimpse of your existence.

AME-NO-MIOYA-GAMI

Hmm...

A

I sincerely, sincerely hope you will give us guidance today to illuminate the future of the new Japanese history. I would really appreciate it if you would give us messages.

AME-NO-MIOYA-GAMI

[*Slowly shakes head left and right with his eyes closed and remains silent for about 10 seconds.*] Hmm... [*About five seconds of silence.*] Ahh... Umm... Ahh... Umm... Ahh... Umm... Ahh... Umm...

UMM... UM MUKUNDAKARA POKOLO ENDORO YOOTOOKO UMM GAERUS TOROMINUKUSURABDARA OKO EN EE WOOTZAI KONTSU AGLOO EE... [*tongues continue*].

A

[*Smiles wryly.*]

AME-NO-MIOYA-GAMI

OIZOROKO KAHBEERU REKKUIYA KUIYARA DOKOROBUSSARADEKO EINYAGAKORA GUDURU OWA ABRUTOKAGAPEKARAKUITTE GOIGOIJIARAPU.

A

Lord Ame-no-Mioya-Gami, thank you very much for your precious words. But I'm afraid there is a language barrier between us, and we are having difficulty understanding your thoughts accurately.

AME-NO-MIOYA-GAMI

BUIYAGAKIKOTSUITEKIKOROPOISSHUJO SHOO TZE SUIKEIKU KOAU! DE GUI SHEEBOTSU DOO SOO DOO CHI KII? KAIYESHOO ROOROOROOROODA... [*tongues continue*].

A

I see. I am starting to understand. You are talking about the time when you created the universe, aren't you?

AME-NO-MIOYA-GAMI

Hmm... YA... OON ISH... SHOO!

A

You opened several doors and let souls go out of them. Something like that?

AME-NO-MIOYA-GAMI

AH, GOOREDIKII, WOOSUROORUSUROOSUROOSUROO
SUROO AA EE WOOIRI ARABUNKIYARAKKEEEDI SUIRYA
SUIYA GOGOARA TEGEBISSHIERAKU.

A

I know, I'm catching on. Somehow, you seem to resemble the
gods of Hinduism (who gave us spiritual messages before).

AME-NO-MIOYA-GAMI

TZARA   GAOUCHIAANO   SHWAERABOBUGHAAI
KUIRI! KUIGRI GUIGUILGUILGUIL DIAGOSEI!

B

With all due respect, are you Vishnu?

AME-NO-MIOYA-GAMI

[*In a rather strong tone.*] NOGEGAGOGOTTETETI
GOOLIN! DADA JISH! AHH! BOCHU SHAISHA!
OUGEURRUIDIGGOHH BUISH!

B

No?

A

Do you remember any Japanese words? I think you have some close connection to...

AME-NO-MIOYA-GAMI

AHH... UZUROOUZU KOHH OONNURU HOUNNOROUUIYOU GUIGUIABORESSHUA BORUSSHUA BOHHWICHAA WITCHAA RUHKYA KWAEIISHUU DOGOGODOGO DODODO KWICHIKORO BOGOROBOGOROTAHH WI!

A

Thank you very much. Do you have any memory of having some connection with Gautama Siddhartha or Shakyamuni Buddha?

AME-NO-MIOYA-GAMI

Hmm...

B

According to our spiritual research, part of El Cantare was born in India 80,000 years ago. Are you that part of El Cantare who was born 80,000 years ago?

AME-NO-MIOYA-GAMI

[*About five seconds of silence.*]

B

You don't know?

A

Just now, I could see that you're not sure [*smiles wryly*].

When Master Ryuho Okawa gave a lecture titled, "Modern Developments in the Spirit World," he talked about a dream he had. In his dream, he soared high up to the summit of Mt. Meru, and there, he was officially recognized as the most venerated of all Indian gods. At that time, he was called "Surya" (refer to *My Journey through the Spirit World* [New York: IRH Press, 2018]). Is there something you can remember about your connection with Surya? Are you unsure about this, too?

Asking about Ame-no-Mioya-Gami's relation to the god of the sky Anu

B

Then, do you know the name "Anu," the god of the sky[2]?

AME-NO-MIOYA-GAMI

[*About three seconds of silence.*] HAA... HAAOO.

A

Descended to the earth? No. I understood that. I'm catching on.

AME-NO-MIOYA-GAMI

[*Clicks tongue.*] AH... HA... UMM... AH... UMM, A... UMM... UMM, UMM, UMM, UMM, UM! A, UMM, UMM, UUMM. UMM... UMMMM! AHH!

A

You seem to be beginning to remember something.

AME-NO-MIOYA-GAMI

[*As if singing while doing various movements with his hands and arms.*] AA, AHH, UMM UMM, UMMM, KUIARAKE, KUIARAKE, KUIARAKE. UMM, KUIARAKE, KUIARAKE, KUIARAKE. UMM. AAANUUU [*drawls for about 10 seconds*]. [*Tongues continue.*]

A

Excuse me, Lord Ame-no-Mioya-Gami. Are you summoning a spirit?

AME-NO-MIOYA-GAMI

OHH AHH UMM.

A

This rhythm is similar to the melody of Japanese Shinto and is rather ethereal.

AME-NO-MIOYA-GAMI

UMM. [*With a different tone.*] UMM MUUH.

A

Is this a tune for summoning spirits? Are you managing the spiritual field or creating a kind of sanctuary? [*About three seconds of silence.*] Are you Lord Anu? [*About three seconds of silence.*] Lord Ame-no-Mioya-Gami...

AME-NO-MIOYA-GAMI

[*Points the right index finger downward twice and waves his right hand in front of his face.*]

A

Are you saying we should go down? Do you mean you descended to the earth? Are you saying that's wrong?

AME-NO-MIOYA-GAMI

[*Crosses his arms in an X in front of his chest.*]

A

Do you mean "wrong"?

AME-NO-MIOYA-GAMI

[*While pointing his right index finger downward.*] AAANUU.

A

Oh, you mean you descended to the earth as (the god of the sky) Anu?

AME-NO-MIOYA-GAMI

[*Crosses his arms in an X in front of his chest.*]

A

So it's wrong [*smiles wryly*].

B

Did you come from outer space?

AME-NO-MIOYA-GAMI

[*Picking up a wet towel from the table.*] AAANUU. [*Puts down the wet towel and puts a glass on top of it.*]

A

Oh, do you mean the soul of Ame-no-Mioya-Gami guided Anu? Your role was to guide from outer space or heaven to the god of the sky Anu, who had descended to Mesopotamia. Is this what you mean?

AME-NO-MIOYA-GAMI

[*Gives small nods repeatedly.*]

C

In that case, am I correct in assuming that you are the Primordial God-like Being or the Primordial Buddha-like Being?

AME-NO-MIOYA-GAMI

[*About 10 seconds of silence while pushing his right temple with the right index finger.*]

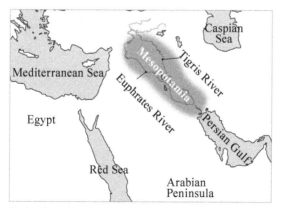

The location of Mesopotamia. The southern area is called Sumer.

3

Giving Spiritual Message Using Hotsuma Characters

Ame-no-Mioya-Gami guided ancient Japan

A

[*Taking out a piece of board.*] Lord Ame-no-Mioya-Gami, please take a look at this. These are the characters used in *Hotsuma Tsutae* that describe ancient Japanese history.

AME-NO-MIOYA-GAMI

[*In a quiet voice.*] Hmm...

A

They are similar to cuneiform characters used in Mesopotamia or Sumer. Do you know these characters?

Part of Awa-uta (song of the mythological age) written in hotsuma characters.

AME-NO-MIOYA-GAMI

[*About five seconds of silence.*] [*Holds out his right hand to receive the board from Interviewer A.*]

* All statements in quotations below are the letters Ame-no-Mioya-Gami pointed out on the board and read out by Interviewer A.

AME-NO-MIOYA-GAMI

[*Points at hotsuma characters on the board in order.*]

"I am Ame-no-Mioya-Gami"

A

I understand. So Lord Ame-no-Mioya-Gami does exist. Thank you very much for coming down here. The fact that you are now communicating with us using the ancient Japanese characters means you guided ancient Japan, is that right?

AME-NO-MIOYA-GAMI

[*Nods.*]

A

Given that you also guided ancient Sumer and other civilizations, and that hotsuma characters are similar to their cuneiform characters, I assume there is some similarity, connection, or close relationship between them.

AME-NO-MIOYA-GAMI

[*Points at hotsuma characters on the board.*]

"God of the universe"

A

Ah, are you the God of the universe?

AME-NO-MIOYA-GAMI

Hm. [*Nods.*]

A

If you are the God of the universe transcending the God of the Earth, you would be a huge existence. Are you such a huge existence?

AME-NO-MIOYA-GAMI

Hm. [*Nods.*]

A

So, Ame-no-Mioya-Gami is the God of the universe. I see. Do you mean the entire universe rather than the heaven of Earth?

AME-NO-MIOYA-GAMI

Hm. [*Nods.*]

Where is Ame-no-Mioya-Gami situated now?

A

Have you ever been born with a physical body? Have you always been in the universe?

AME-NO-MIOYA-GAMI

Hm, hmm. [*Points at hotsuma characters on the board.*]

"Now I am in Andromeda"

A

Oh, so you are the God of Andromeda? You say you are now situated in the Andromeda Nebula. So, did you come from the Andromeda Galaxy today?

AME-NO-MIOYA-GAMI

Hm. [*Nods.*]

A

Thank you very much for traveling such a long distance to come here.

AME-NO-MIOYA-GAMI

Hm. [*Nods.*]

A

When Master Ryuho Okawa conducted spiritual research through space people readings, we discovered that there are some traces in Japanese Shinto that hint at Andromeda. So are you in that same stream?

AME-NO-MIOYA-GAMI

[*Points at hotsuma characters on the board.*]

"The origin of Japanese Shinto is Andromeda"

A

We just have received the message, "The origin of Japanese Shinto is Andromeda."

Ame-no-Mioya-Gami's relation to Amaterasu-O-Mikami and Kuni-no-Tokotachi-no-Kami

A

Did you guide Amaterasu-O-Mikami?

AME-NO-MIOYA-GAMI

[*Points at hotsuma characters on the board*.]

"Amaterasu in the Solar System"

A

"Amaterasu in the Solar System"?

AME-NO-MIOYA-GAMI

Hm, hm. [*Nods*.]

A

Oh, I see. Is she sort of an independent god in the Solar System?

AME-NO-MIOYA-GAMI

Hm. [*Nods*.]

C

Then, how are you related to Kuni-no-Tokotachi-no-Kami?

AME-NO-MIOYA-GAMI

Hmm. [*Points at hotsuma characters on the board*.]

"The Earth"

A

Oh, so Amaterasu-O-Mikami has to do with the Solar System, while Kuni-no-Tokotachi-no-Kami with the Earth. Is that right?

AME-NO-MIOYA-GAMI

Hm. [*Nods.*]

A

And you are in Andromeda, right?

AME-NO-MIOYA-GAMI

Hm, hm, hm, hm, hm. [*Nods.*]

A

I see. Is Kuni-no-Tokotachi-no-Kami a god of Earth then?

AME-NO-MIOYA-GAMI

[*Points at hotsuma characters on the board.*]

"God of agriculture"

A

So, Kuni-no-Tokotachi-no-Kami is the god of agriculture. So he makes sure there is enough rice harvest and makes a country rich in food.

AME-NO-MIOYA-GAMI

Hm. [*Nods.*]

4

The Relationship between El Cantare and Ame-no-Mioya-Gami

Ame-no-Mioya-Gami is the "beginning"

C

If so, how should we understand your relation to Amaterasu-O-Mikami?

AME-NO-MIOYA-GAMI

Hmm... [*Points at hotsuma characters on the board.*]

"I am the beginning"

A

"I am the beginning."

B

Do you mean you are the Original God?

AME-NO-MIOYA-GAMI

Hm, hm. Hm, hm. [*Nods.*]

A

I see. This conversation is on such a large scale, and it is difficult for us to accept it readily. Do you mean you are the beginning of the entire universe?

AME-NO-MIOYA-GAMI

Hm. [*Nods.*]

Ame-no-Mioya-Gami's relation to El Cantare, the God of the Earth

A

It makes me wonder about your relationship with El Cantare.

C

Are we correct in assuming you are part of Lord El Cantare?

AME-NO-MIOYA-GAMI

Hmm. [*Points at hotsuma characters on the board.*]

"El Cantare is part of me"

A

Please wait a minute. Did you say El Cantare is part of you?

AME-NO-MIOYA-GAMI

Hm, hm, hm. [*Nods.*]

A

Then, it sounds like you are above Him...

AME-NO-MIOYA-GAMI

Hm, hm, hm. [*Nods.*]

A

Well... For those of us who have been studying the Happy Science teachings for more than 30 years, this is rather difficult to accept. I'm not sure if we can accept it...

AME-NO-MIOYA-GAMI

[*Points at hotsuma characters on the board.*]

"El Cantare is the God of the Earth"

A

"El Cantare is the God of the Earth."

Which dimension does
Ame-no-Mioya-Gami belong to?

B

In our teachings we have learned about Lord El Cantare as the ninth dimensional existence. We have also learned about El Cantare as a 14th dimensional existence and that Primordial Buddha exists in a much higher place, beyond the 20th dimension.

AME-NO-MIOYA-GAMI

Hmm.

B

So, do you belong to the world beyond the 20th dimension or in a much higher realm beyond our humanly recognition, such as the 50th dimension?

AME-NO-MIOYA-GAMI

Hm, hmm... [*Picks up the digital clock from the desk and points at 11 on display.*]

"11th (dimension)"

A

Do you mean you belong to the 11th dimension? [*Breathing becomes shallower.*] Please wait a minute. We've learned that the ninth dimension is the highest in the Earth's spirit realm, but are you saying the 11th dimension? This is quite difficult for us petty existences to...

Asking Ame-no-Mioya-Gami again about his relation to El Cantare

C

I'm sorry for asking the same question again, but how are you related to Lord El Cantare?

AME-NO-MIOYA-GAMI

Hm... [*Circles his right hand with his left index finger.*]

A

Is He inside a big soul?

AME-NO-MIOYA-GAMI

[*Points at the right thumb with his left index finger.*]

A

So El Cantare would be equivalent to the thumb?

AME-NO-MIOYA-GAMI

Hm. [*Nods.*]

A

Lord Ame-no-Mioya-Gami is the main body, while El Cantare is equivalent to the thumb. Is that what you are saying?

AME-NO-MIOYA-GAMI

Hm. [*Nods.*]

C

Are we correct in assuming you are the core consciousness of Lord El Cantare?

AME-NO-MIOYA-GAMI

Huh? [*Makes a small circle with both hands and then draws a big circle using both arms.*]

A

Are you encompassing Him within your whole body?

AME-NO-MIOYA-GAMI

Hm! [*Nods.*] [*Gets up, walks to the image of halo in the front of the prayer room, and points at its center.*]

A

You are this central point... this is Lord Ame-no-Mioya-Gami?

AME-NO-MIOYA-GAMI

[*Shakes his head.*]

A

What? So you mean El Cantare is the central point.

AME-NO-MIOYA-GAMI

[*Tracing the circumference of the halo with his right hand before returning to the seat.*]

A

And this circumference is Lord Mioya-Gami. Oh... if you use the human body as an analogy, is your relationship to El Cantare like the relationship between the whole body and the heart?

AME-NO-MIOYA-GAMI

Hm...

A

Not necessarily?

AME-NO-MIOYA-GAMI

Hm, hmm...

A

So it's not something comparable to the heart. Are you saying you are a much bigger existence than El Cantare?

AME-NO-MIOYA-GAMI

Hm...

A

Did you say you are the circumference of the large circle with El Cantare at the center?

AME-NO-MIOYA-GAMI

Hm, hm, hm, hm. [*Nods.*]

A

Do you mean El Cantare is part of your soul born on Earth?

AME-NO-MIOYA-GAMI

Hm, hm, hm. [*Nods.*]

A

And your consciousness has traveled from the Andromeda Galaxy and has entered the physical body (of Master Ryuho Okawa), and you said you are an 11th dimensional existence?

AME-NO-MIOYA-GAMI

Hm, hm. [*Nods.*]

A

OK, I understand.

Why did Ame-no-Mioya-Gami come from Andromeda to Earth?

B

You said you are an 11th dimensional existence. Then, what made you decide to come from Andromeda to this Milky Way Galaxy and give guidance?

AME-NO-MIOYA-GAMI

[*Points at hotsuma characters on the board.*]

"Old"

A

"Old." Does this mean Andromeda is older?

AME-NO-MIOYA-GAMI

Hm, hm. [*Nods.*]

A

You don't necessarily mean it's superior, but it's just older in terms of the flow of time. Is that what you are saying?

AME-NO-MIOYA-GAMI

Hmm... [*Points at hotsuma characters on the board.*]

"The Earth is new"

A

I see. "The Earth is new."

AME-NO-MIOYA-GAMI

Hm. [*Nods.*]

C

Master mentioned in the beginning that it may have been a little too late to investigate you. But are we correct in assuming that you came down here today because Earth is in need of existence like you?

AME-NO-MIOYA-GAMI

[*Shakes his right hand.*]

A

No?

AME-NO-MIOYA-GAMI

[*Points at hotsuma characters on the board.*]

"No business"

A

What? Please wait a minute [*laughs*]. After everything you've said, you've suddenly become cold... What do you mean by "no business"? Do you mean you have a different role or mission?

AME-NO-MIOYA-GAMI

Hm. [*Points at hotsuma characters on the board.*]

"None"

A

So you have no business here.

AME-NO-MIOYA-GAMI

[*Points at hotsuma characters on the board.*]

"I've left Earth up to El Cantare"

A

You have left Earth up to El Cantare?

AME-NO-MIOYA-GAMI

Hm. [*Nods.*]

5

Examining the Origin of Japanese Shinto

Was Ame-no-Mioya-Gami born on the earth?

B

In Master Ryuho Okawa's comment earlier, he said he had some doubts about the description in *Hotsuma Tsutae* that says Ame-no-Mioya-Gami had been born on the earth once. You said you are an 11th dimensional existence, but was part of you born in ancient Japan?

AME-NO-MIOYA-GAMI

Hm, hmm... [*About 20 seconds of silence.*] [*Points at hotsuma characters on the board.*]

"People worshiped me a long time ago"

Japan's relation to Africa and India
in ancient times

B

You said you are the God of the universe that belongs to the 11th dimension, and you also say people worshiped you in ancient Japan. So how did people in ancient Japan come to know your existence and write about you in the old document *Hotsuma Tsutae*? In which era was *Hotsuma Tsutae* written, and who wrote it in the first place? Could you tell us about that? The name "Ame-no-Mioya-Gami" had been hidden behind a veil for a very long time, so how come the people in ancient Japan could know your name? Why did they write about you in *Hotsuma Tsutae*?

AME-NO-MIOYA-GAMI

Hm, hmm... [*Points at hotsuma characters on the board.*]

"Lemuria"

A

Oh, it was passed down from Lemuria[3] to Japan.

AME-NO-MIOYA-GAMI

Hm. [*Nods.*]

A

I see... So it wasn't passed down from the Mu continent[4]? Did it go from Lemuria to Mu and then to Japan?

AME-NO-MIOYA-GAMI

Hmm...

A

Was it passed down from Lemuria?

AME-NO-MIOYA-GAMI

Hmm... hm, hm. [*Nods.*]

A

Lemuria... then, is the Japanese civilization linked to Lemuria?

AME-NO-MIOYA-GAMI

Hmm. [*Points at hotsuma characters on the board.*]

"Africa and India were connected"

B

Do you mean the Gonda-Ana continent[5]?

AME-NO-MIOYA-GAMI

Hm, hm, hmm...

B

So it's not Gonda-Ana.

A

It was before the continental drift occurred and the continent separated. Then, after several transitions of civilizations, your name was passed down to Japan.

AME-NO-MIOYA-GAMI

Hmm.

A

So you mean India, Africa, and Japan are spiritually connected? Is there spiritual lineage between them?

AME-NO-MIOYA-GAMI

AMM... UMM BOO AN UMM UM BOO EEN ENMU... OOOOOO... AU UGUCHI DOO IYORAKATEKO JUNDOBO GUNJI SHOO SHOO SHOO ABE IGUNANGO EDISHORO SODEKUTSUWAKA KINDIIGYUARA KOCCHIRABO AHH BOOSHA!

A

[*Laughs.*] Well... I can sense your vibrations, but there is a language barrier, and I just can't understand what you are saying. I'm very sorry!

Was Amaterasu-O-Mikami a male god?

A

There is an important point when considering Japan's national policy and its future. Master Ryuho Okawa was also wondering about this. In Japan, there is a lineage from

Amaterasu-O-Mikami. But in *Hotsuma Tsutae*, there is a description of Amaterasu being a male god. It is probably one of the reasons it is not regarded as an official historical record. Why was she described as male? Was there any reason?

AME-NO-MIOYA-GAMI

Hmm... [*Points at hotsuma characters on the board.*]

"The sun is male in a hot country"

A

Is it because there is an impression that the sun is male in a hot country? Then, is Amaterasu-O-Mikami actually a female god?

AME-NO-MIOYA-GAMI

[*Points at hotsuma characters on the board.*]

"Female in a cold country"

A

"The sun is male in a hot country and female in a cold country."

AME-NO-MIOYA-GAMI

Hm, hm. [*Nods.*]

C

Has Amaterasu-O-Mikami ever been born in Japan as a male emperor?

AME-NO-MIOYA-GAMI

[*About five seconds of silence.*] [*Shrugs.*]

A

You are not sure... I understand that she hasn't. Then, does that mean she was described as a male in terms of concept but was actually born in this world as female?

AME-NO-MIOYA-GAMI

[*Shrugs.*]

A

You don't know. I see.

6

Ame-no-Mioya-Gami's Relation to Vishnu

The relationship between Ame-no-Mioya-Gami and Vishnu

A

Let me ask one more question. I think your answer to this question will have quite a big impact on Earth in the future. India has become a very big country with over 1.3 billion people now. It worships Vishnu as one of the central gods, and we are now investigating our relation to Vishnu.

AME-NO-MIOYA-GAMI

Hm. [*Nods.*]

A

A moment ago, you mentioned that Africa and India were connected. So what is your relation to Vishnu?

AME-NO-MIOYA-GAMI

Hmm... [*Points at hotsuma characters on the board.*]

"Cousin"

A

"Cousin"! If you had a human relationship, Vishnu would be your cousin.

AME-NO-MIOYA-GAMI

Hmm.

A

Comparing the world of God to a human familial relationship, he would be your cousin. There is such a lineage.

AME-NO-MIOYA-GAMI

Hm, hm, hm, hm. [*Nods.*]

A

Did you create many such beings?

AME-NO-MIOYA-GAMI

Hm, hm, hm, hm, hm, hm. [*Nods.*]

The relationship between Ame-no-Mioya-Gami and El Miore, the ruler of Venus

A

[*To the audience.*] Does anyone have any questions?

[*Someone in the audience says, "El Miore[6]."*]

A

OK. Someone asked, "What is your relation to El Miore?"

AME-NO-MIOYA-GAMI

Hmm... [*Points at hotsuma characters on the board.*]

"My right eye"

A

Your right eye? So El Miore is your right eye.

AME-NO-MIOYA-GAMI

Hm. [*Nods.*]

A

Are you sure? El Miore is the ruler of Venus.

AME-NO-MIOYA-GAMI

Hm. [*Nods.*]

A

Really...

B

The scale of this conversation is so big. It's mind-boggling to ordinary human beings like us.

AME-NO-MIOYA-GAMI

[*Points at hotsuma characters on the board.*]

"I am not human"

A

You are not human.

AME-NO-MIOYA-GAMI

Hm, hm. [*Nods.*]

7

About Japan's Next Mission

Egypt, India, and Japan are connected

B

Since you appear in the stream of Japanese Shinto teachings, I would like to ask this question. What is the position of Japanese Shinto, or the teachings of Japanese gods, on this Earth? And what is their mission? Although your name has been hidden, you have now appeared, and different gods of Japanese Shinto have appeared under various guidance. So what is the significance of Japanese Shinto on Earth or in the universe?

AME-NO-MIOYA-GAMI

Hmm... [*Points at hotsuma characters on the board.*]

"Egypt, India, Japan"

A

Do you mean Egypt, India, and Japan are connected straight with each other? Is there a spiritual flow or connection between Egypt, India, and Japan?

AME-NO-MIOYA-GAMI

Hm, hm. [*Nods.*]

A

Huh... so these countries have a close connection with each other.

What is Japan's next mission?

B

Then, am I correct in assuming that on Earth, Japan has a very strong spiritual energy field and is a vital country in a sense to firmly establish faith on Earth?

AME-NO-MIOYA-GAMI

Hm... [*Points at hotsuma characters on the board.*]

"Last"

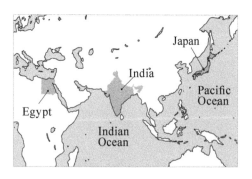

A

Last?

AME-NO-MIOYA-GAMI

Hm. [*Nods.*]

B

Do you mean this is the last chance?

AME-NO-MIOYA-GAMI

Hm, hm, hm. [*Nods.*]

A

Or, you mean it's the end?

AME-NO-MIOYA-GAMI

Hm. [*Nods.*]

A

Hold on. Would you give us another hint?

AME-NO-MIOYA-GAMI

Hmm... [*Points at hotsuma characters on the board.*]

"Next is the universe"

A

"Next is the universe." From Egypt, India, to Japan, and the next is the universe. Are you saying we should open the gate to a space civilization?

AME-NO-MIOYA-GAMI

Hm. [*Nods.*]

Will human beings leave Earth?

A

Ah, that's why you are making the spiritual current flow from Andromeda today.

On October 10, 2015, our movie titled *The Laws of the Universe – Part 0* will be released nationwide in Japan with Master Ryuho Okawa as its executive producer. So are you expecting us to enlighten people in Japan—an underdeveloped country in terms of UFOs and a country that has limited information on outer space?

AME-NO-MIOYA-GAMI

[*Points at hotsuma characters on the board.*]

"Too small"

A

The scale of such talk was too small. I am really sorry.

You said, "Next is the universe." Does this mean Earth should change and shift to space civilization?

AME-NO-MIOYA-GAMI

[*Shakes his head.*]

A

No?

AME-NO-MIOYA-GAMI

Hm... [*Points at hotsuma characters on the board.*]

"Leave"

A

You mean the earthlings will leave Earth?

AME-NO-MIOYA-GAMI

Hm. [*Nods.*]

A

But according to the teachings of Master Ryuho Okawa, the sun will keep burning for the next five billion years, and the

Earth's environment is allowed to exist as the ground for soul training. Do you mean some will leave Earth while others will remain here? Or will Earth die out, and will everyone on Earth migrate to other planets?

AME-NO-MIOYA-GAMI

Ah... hm... [*Points at hotsuma characters on the board.*]

"Stupid"

A

"Stupid"? [*Laughs.*] [*The audience laughs.*] Well...

[*To Interviewer C.*] Is there any other question?

C

We apologize. What you are saying is on quite a large scale, so we can't talk on the same level. We would really appreciate it if you could give some advice to Happy Science, especially our followers.

AME-NO-MIOYA-GAMI

Hmm... [*About 15 seconds of silence.*] [*Points at hotsuma characters on the board.*]

"Out"

A

We've received the revelation, "Out." Does it mean we are already "out" or we are heading in the direction of going "out"?

AME-NO-MIOYA-GAMI

[*Points at hotsuma characters on the board.*]

"Stupid"

A

Round two... [*Laughs.*] [*The audience laughs.*] I'm beginning to kind of understand as if I am solving a Zen riddle. Are you trying to tell us that Earth is facing serious danger? Or are you deeply disappointed? I sense a stern reprimand behind your words because we haven't yet accomplished our mission.

AME-NO-MIOYA-GAMI

[*About five seconds of silence.*] [*Turning both palms upward.*]

A

OK. I see.

AME-NO-MIOYA-GAMI

[*Turns his left palm upward in front of his body and puts his right thumb upward.*]

A

What is that? Is there a meaning to such a mudra-like gesture?

AME-NO-MIOYA-GAMI

[*Points at Hotsuma characters on the board.*]

"I want to leave"

A

"You want to leave." [*The audience laughs.*] I understand! We can't place a greater spiritual burden on you. We apologize for making you talk with such ordinary people—such fools like us. I am really sorry.

Thank you very much for coming all the way from the Andromeda Galaxy to the prayer room of Happy Science General Headquarters in Japan on Earth. Thank you very much for giving us guidance today.

RYUHO OKAWA

[*Claps loudly twice, and then claps several times.*] OK.

8

Ame-no-Mioya-Gami Seems to Have Been Away from Earth

Ame-no-Mioya-Gami is mainly based in Andromeda

RYUHO OKAWA

He seems to be greater than we imagined. He is not a human. It does seem like he was not born as a human.

A

Right.

RYUHO OKAWA

What he said was simple and big, so it is difficult to understand. But that's how it seems to be. When Ame-no-Mioya-Gami had influence, it seems that Earth was not the way it is today. So it was a much more ancient time.

The beginning of humanity is still very difficult to understand. What kind of being was he? Was he involved in it? Such stories have nothing to do with modern people, so maybe he thought it would be pointless to talk about it. I am not so sure about that.

A

I felt I was listening to the story of the modern version of *Kojiki*.

RYUHO OKAWA

It was bigger than *Kojiki*. He is most probably even greater than Allah and Yahweh. I think he is a much greater existence.

A

Yes. It is incredibly large scale.

RYUHO OKAWA

After all, I think Earth is just a footstep to him. The Andromeda Galaxy is much more extensive than the Milky Way Galaxy containing Earth. It is said that Andromeda is approaching our galaxy and will eventually merge with ours. Because they are moving toward us, our galaxy may have some "tractive force."

A

I see.

RYUHO OKAWA

Andromeda will eventually merge with this galaxy containing Earth. It is predicted to occur in about four billion years. For this reason, he may be appearing now with Earth as something like a front-line base.

A

Indeed, I've recently seen some science magazines featuring the possible collision crisis between the Andromeda Galaxy and our Galaxy in the distant future.

RYUHO OKAWA

Well, rather than a crisis of collision, it's more like...

A

Being swallowed up?

RYUHO OKAWA

Suppose Andromeda is centrifuged, our Galaxy will be at its outer edge. So, I don't think it's something like being swallowed up.

In their eyes, 100 million years probably feel like one day, so our small-scale missionary work, elections, and movies may seem like stories of one small country within the Earth's Spirit World.

We can obtain information on planets closer to Earth (through our space readings), but we have little information about Andromeda. So, I think there are deeper secrets. So far, we have only found two or three people who had come to Earth from Andromeda.

A

Yes. In our readings, there are very few people whose souls had originally lived in the Andromeda Galaxy.

RYUHO OKAWA

I think it (the Andromeda Galaxy) is old. Many seem to come to Earth through other planets closer to Earth, so there may be few souls that had lived only in Andromeda.

The origin of the Japanese gods is quite ancient

A

He mentioned the current that exists on Earth—from Egypt, India, and to Japan.

RYUHO OKAWA

Well, his story is on such a large scale, so I don't know what to make of it. Based on what he said, I feel he is still over there.

A

You mean in Andromeda. He certainly seems like a spiritual consciousness that is very far away.

RYUHO OKAWA

Today, Ame-no-Mioya-Gami couldn't speak Japanese, which means he has been away from Earth for a while.

A

I'm glad we had this board. [*The audience laughs.*] We made it three minutes before entering this prayer room.

RYUHO OKAWA

I think this means he does not directly guide Japan. From this, it seems clear that the origin of the Japanese gods is quite ancient. I presume the Japanese civilization is the descendant of an orthodox civilization that came from the universe.

A

I see.

RYUHO OKAWA

So Ame-no-Mioya-Gami is more than just an earlier emperor who had roots in Japanese Shinto.

A

Yes. He said He is the Primordial God or the "beginning." He has a Primordial Will.

Toward the "Laws of the Universe" and the "Laws of El Cantare"

RYUHO OKAWA

The story about ancient continents is too long, so I haven't managed to describe it enough. Well, it may have nothing to do with modern people, though.

A

Right.

RYUHO OKAWA

It may sound irrelevant for those who still don't know whether there is an afterworld. But when the time comes, such a story may come up. When the door to the "Laws of the Universe" opens, and when everyone can see and come to believe in space people and want to know the history of Earth, such stories may come up. Perhaps, after I return to the other world, the "Laws of El Cantare" may truly start to come down. I can speak "Earth's language," so I may be able to give them to you.

Anyway, we still don't know who exactly Ame-no-Mioya-Gami is, but at least we know he had come from Andromeda.

A

It became clear that He had some connection to Japan as well. We also learned that Amaterasu-O-Mikami is the goddess of the Solar System.

RYUHO OKAWA

Well, it wasn't really a spiritual message, but more like "kokkuri-san" (similar to Ouija board) [*laughs*]. I had some dubious feeling beforehand. It turns out that he seems to be in a place where he cannot come to give us his message directly.

A

Yes.

RYUHO OKAWA

His story sounded quite far from us. But I think he will appear again when the time comes.

A

We will wait for the opportunity while making efforts on our part.

RYUHO OKAWA

OK. [*Claps once.*]

A

Thank you very much.

EDITOR'S NOTES

1 Space people reading

Retrieving the memory of an alien soul that had come from outer space and has now reincarnated on Earth as an earthling. Okawa has the ability to draw out the soul's memory as an extraterrestrial being and have him or her talk in that consciousness (refer to *Alien Invasion* [Tokyo: HS Press, 2015]).

2 Anu, the god of the sky

The supreme god of the ancient Sumer. According to the spiritual research of Happy Science, it is the same being as El Cantare, the God of the Earth.

3 Lemuria

The ancient continent that existed in the Indian Ocean (also called Ramudia). According to the spiritual research of Happy Science, the continent appeared 86,000 years ago and the civilization that mainly focused on arts flourished from 44,000 years ago. Although the continent sank 27,000 years ago, a part of the civilization was passed on to the Mu continent, which, at that time, was the colony of Lemuria (refer to *The Laws of the Sun* [New York: IRH Press, 2018]).

4 The Mu continent

The legendary continent that existed in the Pacific Ocean. According to the spiritual research of Happy Science, the great king, Ra Mu built the golden age of the Mu civilization about 17,000 years ago. However, about 15,300 years ago, the Mu continent sank into the ocean in three stages (refer to *The Laws of the Sun*).

5 The Gonda-Ana continent

Interviewer B is referring to the Garna continent revealed in *The Laws of the Sun*. According to the spiritual reading of Happy Science, it was the continent that rose from the sea 962,000 years ago after an underwater volcanic eruption which caused the seabed to rise. It is said to have been located in the area between the present-day African and South American continents. The Garna civilization that mainly focused on supernatural powers flourished 760,000 years ago (refer to *The Laws of the Sun*).

6 El Miore

The grand spirit who is said to have existed before humanity was created on Earth. He is the one who created the Venusian civilization. Later, He became the very first personified grand spirit on Earth and changed His name to El Cantare (refer to *The Laws of the Sun*).

CHAPTER TWO

The Descent of Ame-no-Mioya-Gami

Tracing Back the Roots of the Japanese Civilization

Originally recorded in Japanese on July 23, 2018
at Special Lecture Hall, Happy Science, Japan
and later translated into English.

Interviewers from Happy Science

Shio Okawa[*]
Aide to Master & CEO

The two other interviewers are symbolized as A and B.

---

[*] *Her professional title represents her position at the time of the interview.*

1

Ame-no-Mioya-Gami, Still Covered in Mystery

The aim of this spiritual message is to reveal who Ame-no-Mioya-Gami is

RYUHO OKAWA

Today (July 23, 2018), I would like to receive a spiritual message from Ame-no-Mioya-Gami under the title, "The Descent of Ame-no-Mioya-Gami." When we previously summoned Ame-no-Mioya-Gami to Happy Science General Headquarters (on October 3, 2015, "Who Is Ame-no-Mioya-Gami?" was recorded. Chapter One), he didn't speak Japanese, so it was an unusual session. (Note: Because Ame-no-Mioya-Gami did not freely speak Japanese, we used a board with ancient Japanese hotsuma characters and had him point to the letters to communicate.) Apparently, he was on another planet at the time, and because he was summoned suddenly, he could not adjust himself to speaking in Japanese. Now it seems he has "come back to Japan," so we are able to communicate with him in Japanese.

From around August or September this year (2018), we are planning to shoot the movie, *Immortal Hero* (executive producer and original story by Ryuho Okawa). We changed the main character's name from the one used in the original story to Makoto Mioya, which was taken from Ame-no-Mioya-Gami. But because the name Mioya sounds unfamiliar to many people, I thought some explanation was necessary to help people understand the significance of that name. So I decided to clarify who Ame-no-Mioya-Gami is, as well as his origin, his connection to Japan, his appearance, and his thoughts. I also want to reveal how he sees Japan and what his position is. I would like people to learn about Ame-no-Mioya-Gami before the screening of the movie.

Only spiritual messages can tell the truth about what is not recorded in history

RYUHO OKAWA

Happy Science is aiming to become a world religion, and we often say that the names of God from various global religions are another name for El Cantare. So what about the God in Japanese Shinto? According to the post-war historical view in particular, the gods of Japanese Shinto have mostly been regarded as ethnic gods. But if this were true, it would not be clear why a world religion should originate in Japan.

Regarding to the Sun Goddess Amaterasu-O-Mikami, who is said to be the ruling deity of Japanese Shinto, I published a book *Ohirume-no-Muchi no Reigen* (literally, "The Spiritual Message from Ohirume-no-Muchi") at the beginning of this year (2018). Ohirume-no-Muchi is another difficult, unfamiliar name. The name actually appears in *Nihon Shoki* and is said to be another name for Amaterasu-O-Mikami.

Various gods appear in both *Kojiki* and *Nihon Shoki*. Although this depends on how it is counted, Amaterasu-O-Mikami is the 96th god to appear if she is the daughter of the god Izanagi. I, myself, have not precisely counted it, but it is strange for the 96th god to be the ruling deity of Japan. Perhaps this is because an effort was made to establish faith in Amaterasu-O-Mikami when *Kojiki* and *Nihon Shoki* were compiled. Empress Jito assumed the throne at that time, so establishing faith in Amaterasu-O-Mikami was probably necessary to legitimize ruling by a female emperor. Even so, there had to be a good reason to establish faith in Amaterasu, so there must be some legends related to this faith.

Even regarding Emperor Jimmu, the first emperor of Japan who made a military expedition to the eastern lands, his time does not go back further than 2,700 years ago. So I have hypothesized that the roots of faith in Amaterasu could go back even prior to that age. That's why I summoned Ohirume-no-Muchi on New Year's Day this year to ask about this point. According to what she said, the Japanese archipelago known as Oyashima began detaching from the continent and coming to form the Japanese archipelago at least 200,000 years ago, or even 300,000 years ago. She said that the Japanese archipelago began separating from the continent in such ancient times and became modernized about 30,000 years ago.

This was an amazing story. This information does not exist in recorded history, but if it is true that Japan became modernized about 30,000 years ago, Japanese history, which is now believed to be about 3,000 years long, accounts for only one-tenth of its true history. It only accounts for the lattermost part of history. This means *Kojiki* and *Nihon Shoki* do not even cover one-third of the late period of Japanese history. Both *Kojiki* and *Nihon Shoki* were compiled in the 700s, so there is no way of knowing about such ancient records. So, I believe only spiritual messages can tell the truth about what is not recorded in mythological history.

Nihon Shoki is a history book while *Kojiki* is a book of myths

RYUHO OKAWA

The Japanese myths are mainly written in *Kojiki* and *Nihon Shoki*, but *Kojiki* is said to contain more mythological aspects.

Kojiki and *Nihon Shoki* were compiled around the same time; *Kojiki* in AD 712 and *Nihon Shoki* in AD 720. While *Nihon Shoki* has far more volumes, *Kojiki* contains more mythological stories.

If I were to compare the texts with documents written on modern Japanese 400-character manuscript paper, *Kojiki* is about 150 pages long. Since *Kojiki* consists of three volumes, each volume would be about 50 pages long. On the other hand, *Nihon Shoki* consists of 30 volumes. But the mythological part consists of only about 70 pages on 400-character manuscript paper. This is probably shorter than one of my hour-long lectures. It has more descriptions of the history of successive emperors and less on mythological matters. For this reason, *Nihon Shoki* is generally considered as a history book while *Kojiki* is a book of myths.

Hotsuma Tsutae is said to have existed before *Kojiki* and *Nihon Shoki*

RYUHO OKAWA

In fact, there is another historical record called *Hotsuma Tsutae* that existed before *Kojiki* and *Nihon Shoki*. It was written in hotsuma characters, which have mostly been forgotten now.

Sometimes, unfamiliar ancient characters are discovered in various archaeological sites, and hotsuma characters are similar to these.

One theory says *Hotsuma Tsutae* was written by Takenouchi-no-Sukune[1]. It is said that he lived a long life (Note: about 300 years). But because it is hard to believe that a person could live for such a long time, some say it was probably a pseudonym that was succeeded for generations. Just like the name Kichiemon Nakamura which is succeeded by *kabuki* actors, the name Takenouchi-no-Sukune is said to have been succeeded for generations. It seems that *Takenouchi Monjo* ("Takenouchi Document") or some historical record like *Hotsuma Tsutae*, written by Takenouchi-no-Sukune the first, was passed down for generations within the Takenouchi family.

Kojiki and *Nihon Shoki* were compiled in favor of the central government at the time

RYUHO OKAWA

Nihon Shoki was written in classical Chinese. This is because the document was intended to be sent to China and have it recognized as the standard history book of Japan. It was sent to the Tang Dynasty of China as a history book so that Japan could be recognized as a modern nation. That was the reason *Nihon Shoki* was written in classical Chinese. *Kojiki*, on the other hand, was written not in classical Chinese but in both *kanji* characters and the *yamato* language (a variant of classical Chinese used in *Manyo-shu* [collection of *waka*, or ancient Japanese poetry]), so it probably was not intended to be sent to China.

Apparently, *Kojiki* and *Nihon Shoki* were compiled based on the many *Fudoki*, or the local history books which existed in various places. But it is said that because *Kojiki* and *Nihon Shoki* were compiled in favor of the central government at the time, a considerable number of descriptions about the history of the local ruling families that did not obey the government were omitted.

It is also said even the names of gods that were very popular in folk religion were omitted from *Kojiki* and *Nihon Shoki*. One example is Sukunahikona-no-Mikoto. He was a very small god who rode on a small leaf boat. He was actually a "superhero" in ancient folklore. He was about the size of the American hero Ant-Man that appears in the *Avengers* movies. He would appear on a small boat and do great work. Apparently, there was a very strong belief in Sukunahikona-no-Mikoto, but because he was from around the Izumo region, he was disparaged and described as an unfamiliar god in both *Kojiki* and *Nihon Shoki*. It is said he may have been "erased." Many descriptions were apparently "erased" in this way, so it has generally been considered that the central government back then tried to justify its rule through the two documents.

The original Japanese characters are more ancient than cuneiform characters and hieroglyphics

RYUHO OKAWA

Hotsuma Tsutae is regarded as an unofficial document and is not considered an official history book. It describes the history of Japanese gods in the "Japanese language" rather than in kanji characters or *kana* (syllabary) characters of the yamato language. In other words, it was written in the characters that were used even before kanji characters and kana characters were introduced to Japan. In this respect, it is very worthy of attention. I don't know how people are able to read them, but perhaps it was successfully passed down through oral tradition.

Hotsuma characters are completely different from the kanji characters or the characters used in South and North Korea. If there are any similar characters, they would be cuneiform characters used in areas around Mesopotamia and hieroglyphics (a writing system using picture symbols) inscribed inside the pyramids of ancient Egypt. Hotsuma characters are slightly similar to these characters. But I suspect hotsuma characters to be much older than those characters. I think there is a possibility that cuneiform characters and hieroglyphs had derived from hotsuma characters.

So, there were characters unique to Japan. The original Japanese language had probably existed, but characters must have been introduced at some point.

As a side note, the cuneiform characters used in the Code of Hammurabi in Mesopotamia are said to have been invented during the ancient Sumerian civilization. There is clearly a legend saying that the language was imparted from outer space to the people in the Sumerian civilization. There is even a record saying this language was taught by aliens (Oannes) who were half-fish, half-human. So it is understood that space people had brought various things to Earth, including language and beer. According to the spiritual research of Happy Science, Thoth[2] taught the characters of ancient Egypt and created various academic studies. In any case, it is very difficult to trace the roots of these things.

Why is it necessary to investigate Ame-no-Mioya-Gami now?

RYUHO OKAWA

Reading *Hotsuma Tsutae* will only confuse you, so today, I will just mention that such a book exists and will directly explore its roots. Ame-no-Mioya-Gami certainly appears in *Hotsuma Tsutae*, and he imparted characters and other knowledge to people, but nothing beyond that is revealed.

In our movie, *Immortal Hero*, the main character's name is Makoto Mioya. So I felt the need to explain Ame-no-Mioya-Gami because those who watch the movie may not understand who Makoto Mioya is. That's why we have come to hold this session.

Hotsuma Tsutae was apparently written by Takenouchi-no-Sukune the First, but I, too, find it difficult to understand. So I'm going to trace further back in history and investigate a much more ancient time. Ohirume-no-Muchi says in her spiritual message that she lived in a physical body on the Japanese archipelago about 5,000 to 6,000 years ago, so we can expect to find much older roots than that. I think we will be able to see Japan's position and significance in relation to the ancient civilizations and space civilizations.

Summoning Ame-no-Mioya-Gami

RYUHO OKAWA

Incidentally, Ms. Shio, Aide to Master & CEO, said she clearly saw Ame-no-Mioya-Gami Shrine in her dream around dawn yesterday. In the dream, she was visiting the shrine when Ame-no-Mioya-Gami descended from the direction near the mountains of the shrine. The shrine was similar to those found in Kyoto and Nara, and there were two wide wooden corridors in parallel (raised floor style) with some space like a garden in the middle. Ame-no-Mioya-Gami walked down this middle pathway, as is often said the Japanese gods do, and descended from the top of the mountain. Ms. Shio was with other people in the corridors; they all welcomed him by bowing and joining their hands together in prayer. She said she only expected to pray and worship him, but Ame-no-Mioya-Gami suddenly stopped and gave a sermon, so she also listened to his teachings. According to her, his body was as large as a statue of *Kongo Rikishi* (guardian deity of Buddha). She could not see his face, but it was probably because she was bowing with her hands in prayer. She may have had such dreams before, but yesterday, she actually heard his words.

I believe such a report means he wants to make his appearance. This could lead to the rewriting of Japanese history.

114

Of course, this may not be something ordinary scholars can easily believe, but I think it will be more credible than the Japanese occult monthly magazine *MU*. In any case, I believe this will be a primary source material and the best material of its kind, so it must be passed down to future generations. As always, I would like to reveal his true nature in the form of a question-and-answer session.

That's it for the introductory remarks.

Now, I will summon him.

[Joins hands in prayer with his eyes closed and rubs his hands.]

O Ame-no-Mioya-Gami.

O Ame-no-Mioya-Gami.

The statue of Kongo Rikishi at the Great South Gate of Todai-ji temple (in Nara Prefecture).

Would you come down to Happy Science and reveal your appearance, your thoughts, and your teachings?

O Ame-no-Mioya-Gami.

O Ame-no-Mioya-Gami.

Would you come down to Happy Science and reveal your inner thoughts?

Please.

[*About 10 seconds of silence.*]

2

Ame-no-Mioya-Gami Descended to Japan 30,000 Years Ago

"I am the Father God of the Japanese race"

AME-NO-MIOYA-GAMI

I'm Ame-no-Mioya-Gami.

A

Lord Ame-no-Mioya-Gami, thank you very much for coming down today.

AME-NO-MIOYA-GAMI

Hmm.

A

We heard that Aide to Master & CEO Shio Okawa also received a message from you in her dream yesterday (July 22, 2018). We would appreciate it if you could first tell us the meaning of the message in her dream from yesterday.

AME-NO-MIOYA-GAMI

Well, it is your job to interpret the dream.

A

I'm sorry. We will try to understand her dream ourselves from now on.

The name "Ame-no-Mioya-Gami" has been passed down, but there is no other information on you, including the shrines that worship you. The last time you came here, you came from outer space at short notice, so we could not grasp the whole picture (Chapter One). So first, we would like to confirm your connection to Japan. What is your connection to Japan? I'd appreciate it if you could start by talking about this.

AME-NO-MIOYA-GAMI

You can think of me as the Father God of the Japanese race.

A

Is that so?

AME-NO-MIOYA-GAMI

Yes.

A

According to Ohirume-no-Muchi, Japan became modernized about 30,000 years ago, and the Japanese archipelago had separated from the continent by at least about 200,000 years ago. Since when have you influenced Japan?

AME-NO-MIOYA-GAMI

Well... in terms of the era that led to the modern civilization, it was about 30,000 years ago.

A

Thirty thousand years ago?

AME-NO-MIOYA-GAMI

My descent to Japan 30,000 years ago made a big difference.

A

So you descended to Japan?

AME-NO-MIOYA-GAMI

Yes.

The Japanese archipelago was almost formed about 200,000 years ago

A

So, am I correct in assuming you descended to Earth with a physical body when the Japanese archipelago was almost formed?

AME-NO-MIOYA-GAMI

The Japanese archipelago had separated from China and Russia and was almost formed about 200,000 to 300,000 years ago... well, 200,000 years ago to be precise. There were still mountains around the area where Okinawa and Taiwan are.

A

I see.

AME-NO-MIOYA-GAMI

A part of that area sank into the sea, and the remaining parts formed islands. So, the landform changed slightly, but Japan was completely detached from the continent.

A

Is that so? At that time, the Mu continent did not even exist, so Ra Mu[3] had not yet appeared on the earth. Is that right?

AME-NO-MIOYA-GAMI

Yes. Ra Mu is much younger than I am.

A

Right. So if you were born 30,000 years ago, before the time of Ra Mu, does this mean you are part of El Cantare's plan and are one of His branch spirits?

AME-NO-MIOYA-GAMI

The currently accepted theory says that the Japanese archipelago was connected to China and that people, rice farming techniques, and other cultures came to Japan from China. A professor at the University of Tokyo once said that the ancestors of the Japanese Imperial Family are Eurasian nomads who came from China via the Korean Peninsula to occupy Japan, but this is wrong.

A

I see.

AME-NO-MIOYA-GAMI

This is not true. It's wrong. By about 200,000 years ago, the Japanese archipelago had completely separated from the continent, and people already lived there. Ohirume-no-Muchi used the expression "modernized" to describe Japan (in her spiritual message); it means a civilization that leads to the modern civilization began to show rapid development about 30,000 years ago.

A

I understand.

Lemuria and Mu were connected before they became separated and then sank

A

We would like to start by clarifying the roots of the Japanese people and the start of the Japanese archipelago. I heard that in those times, there was a continent near India called Ramudia (Lemuria), where the Ramudia (Lemuria) civilization flourished. I think there was also the Mu continent. What were the relations between those continents and civilizations, and the Japanese people and the Japanese civilization 30,000 years ago?

AME-NO-MIOYA-GAMI

Well... the Mu continent and the Lemuria continent, which people today call the Lemuria (Ramudia) civilization, are often confused and regarded as the same. Some historians of ancient history say that Lemuria and Mu are the same, but the fact is, the shape of those continents changed with the times due to the sinking of the continent and other natural disasters. The shape of Mu also changed, and I think what you are talking about is the last stage of the Mu continent. A continent called "Lemuria" or "Ramudia" had also existed in between India and the southern part of Southwest Asia, and it was once connected to Mu in ancient times.

A

Is that so? Mu and Ramudia were connected to each other...

AME-NO-MIOYA-GAMI

But parts of it sank into the sea in several stages, and the continent became separated. Although people say the Indian civilization came from the Lemuria civilization or the current Asian civilization came from the Mu civilization, these civilizations significantly overlapped with each other, and the situation was different depending on the time, so it is difficult to say clearly.

What is considered "Lemuria" had a considerable influence on Africa as well. So your understanding of it is a little different.

When these continents sank, India became a subcontinent leading to the forming of the Himalayas. It was a time when the "wrinkles" on the Earth's surface moved, causing the shape of the land to change. It is difficult to give a detailed explanation about all of this.

A

I understand.

The relation between the hotsuma characters and the cuneiform characters

A

In Master Ryuho Okawa's comments at the beginning, he mentioned the connection between the hotsuma characters and the cuneiform characters of Mesopotamia. Were the hotsuma characters used 30,000 years ago?

AME-NO-MIOYA-GAMI

Do you mean in Japan?

A

Yes. In Japan.

AME-NO-MIOYA-GAMI

Well... it was actually not an Earth-born language. I taught people a space language [*laughs*].

A

You were the one who taught it?

AME-NO-MIOYA-GAMI

Yes. First, I taught them a space language because we needed to enlighten people and create a new civilization. It all started from there.

A

I see.

AME-NO-MIOYA-GAMI

The language gradually changed with time, but it was originally a space language.

A

Is that so? Then, did the cuneiform characters used in Sumer also come from space?

AME-NO-MIOYA-GAMI

Yes, they did.

A

I see. Did one of these languages come first and was then passed on to the other place?

AME-NO-MIOYA-GAMI

Hmm... It's as difficult as confirming which of the planet civilization originated first.

A

Right.

AME-NO-MIOYA-GAMI

They also influenced each other. There is an issue of which was first, so it is very difficult to answer.

A

I see.

AME-NO-MIOYA-GAMI

Well, I think my influence most probably was first.

A

You were the first to introduce the characters then.

AME-NO-MIOYA-GAMI

Yes.

Ame-no-Mioya-Gami flew down to the foothills of Mt. Fuji with a large fleet carrying 200,000 people

A

In that case, is it correct to assume that you flew right down to the Japanese archipelago from outer space?

AME-NO-MIOYA-GAMI

Right. All the ancient Japanese gods have the word "Ame" (in their names), right?

A

Yes.

AME-NO-MIOYA-GAMI

"Ame" means "sky" or "universe."

A

I'd like to ask about the situation in which you flew down to Japan. How big was your fleet? Or did you travel as a spirit body? I would appreciate it if you could tell us the details.

AME-NO-MIOYA-GAMI

Ordinary people only look at the ground. They look at the ground and what is in front of them, but they rarely look up. The fact that the names of the ancient Japanese gods contain the word "Ame" is proof they had come down from the sky.

As for the location, well, I think it was around the center of Japan today. So it must have been near Tokyo, where Mt. Fuji was visible.

A

Mt. Fuji?

AME-NO-MIOYA-GAMI

Yes, Mt. Fuji is the most... From outer space, Mt. Fuji stands out the most.

A

I see.

AME-NO-MIOYA-GAMI

We saw Mt. Fuji as the center, or the core of Japan, and landed on a place where Mt. Fuji could be seen. I think it was on the side of Shizuoka Prefecture.

Mt. Fuji, viewed from south, from Fuji City of Shizuoka Prefecture.

A

Somewhere on the side of Shizuoka Prefecture where Mt. Fuji could be seen?

AME-NO-MIOYA-GAMI

Yes.

A

So you landed on the side of the ocean?

AME-NO-MIOYA-GAMI

Yes, on the southern side. We landed near the foothills of Mt. Fuji.

A

Was it a large fleet?

AME-NO-MIOYA-GAMI

Hmm... how many people came with me? [*About 10 seconds of silence.*] I think about 200,000 people came with me.

A

Two hundred thousand people?

AME-NO-MIOYA-GAMI

Yes.

A

I see.

B

Do you mean you came in a physical body?

AME-NO-MIOYA-GAMI

Hmm. We are technically "aliens." We had to teach the people of Japan on Earth about language, culture, and civilization.

The appearance of Ame-no-Mioya-Gami when he came to Earth

B

If you would allow such a question, I'd like to ask about what you and everyone else on the fleet looked like when you descended to Earth from outer space.

AME-NO-MIOYA-GAMI

Ms. Shio should be asking this question.

SHIO OKAWA

I'm sorry. What did you look like?

AME-NO-MIOYA-GAMI

I appeared in a form you like.

SHIO OKAWA

In a form I like?

AME-NO-MIOYA-GAMI

Yes.

SHIO OKAWA

As a panda?

A&B

In black and white?

AME-NO-MIOYA-GAMI

No, hahaha [*laughs*]. You say such simple things.

SHIO OKAWA

[*Laughs.*] Do you mean you looked like how you appeared in my dream?

AME-NO-MIOYA-GAMI

Hmm. We also have... People of Vega[4] are known to transform their figures, but they are not the only ones with such abilities. When we descended to Earth, we changed our bodies to fit the environment of Earth to some extent. We had to make sure not to frighten the earthlings too much, but at the same time, we had to look like great figures.

The kind of men you prefer would look like naked *yokozuna* (grand champion sumo wrestlers), wouldn't they?

SHIO OKAWA

Oh, I see. Then, do you look like a sumo wrestler and have a rather muscular build?

AME-NO-MIOYA-GAMI

Hmm... In reality, we used to put on various things, but to the people of ancient Japan, it probably looked as if we were wearing wrapped cloth much like *Fujin* (wind god) and *Raijin* (thunder god).

3

The Teachings of Ame-no-Mioya-Gami

Ame-no-Mioya-Gami taught people the custom of bowing with their hands together in prayer

SHIO OKAWA

I'm sorry for bringing up my dream, but you were much bigger than the ordinary people, and you also had an air of strictness or sternness.

AME-NO-MIOYA-GAMI

That's right.

SHIO OKAWA

I had an impression you were similar to a sumo wrestler or a statue of Kongo Rikishi (see p.115). But I couldn't see your face and...

AME-NO-MIOYA-GAMI

I taught people to bow. I often told them not to look me directly in the face because they would "be blinded" if they did.

A

So bowing started from there.

AME-NO-MIOYA-GAMI

I taught people the custom of bowing with their hands together in prayer as part of the Japanese roots. Well, it was partly because I was tall. Mostly, people would kneel on both knees and sit on their heels; they would not raise their faces unless they were told to do so. They were not allowed to see my face. They could only hear my voice echoing from above.

Our voice... we could of course use our actual voice, but it sounded like a telepathic message to them. That's how they understood us.

The teachings of Ame-no-Mioya-Gami, given in ancient Japan

SHIO OKAWA

I'm afraid this is also from my dream, but you were addressing the people in my dream. But because we were very surprised by your appearance and were preoccupied by bowing and quickly sitting closer to you, I couldn't hear your words. Would you tell us what your teachings were when you first landed in Japan?

Teaching 1) Manners

AME-NO-MIOYA-GAMI

Well, there were many things I taught. As you can see, Japan has a wood culture. The shrines were built with wood, which was why they didn't remain. The people worked together to build the shrines.

You (Shio Okawa) closely observed the unique characteristic, which is the basis of Japanese Shinto. That is, the gods walk in the middle of the path to the shrine while people are allowed to walk on either side of the path. So "the middle of the path" is only for gods to walk. This is true for Ise Jingu Shrine and also Meiji Jingu Shrine. Only the gods can indeed walk in the middle of the path. These are the manners we taught. So people moved to either side of the path to sit and listen.

We first taught them manners. We taught the proper manners to show respect to older people and people in higher positions by bowing, putting your hands together in prayer, or sitting on your heels.

Teaching 2) The difference between heaven and earth

AME-NO-MIOYA-GAMI

I often taught about the difference between heaven and earth. I taught that heaven means the sky and that the world of gods exists beyond the sky. I also taught that humans born on earth must accept this world as their place to live and do their best to create a better paradise there.

Teaching 3) Harmony between man and woman

AME-NO-MIOYA-GAMI

There were already men and women, so I taught them about the harmony between man and woman.

Teaching 4) Holding ceremonies at various turning points in life

AME-NO-MIOYA-GAMI

What is more, I taught that people should visit the shrine to hold ceremonies at each turning point in life—such as when they get married, have children, reach adulthood, and get old, die and hold a funeral—and have the gods recognize their growth as their witnesses.

Teaching 5) Ritual prayers and festivals

AME-NO-MIOYA-GAMI

We also encouraged people to perform *kigan* or ritual prayers. In this world, there were times when many battles were fought, or when the harvest was scarce due to unseasonable weather or not enough prey or fish could be caught. So we had them perform kigan and make it a custom to hold festivals every now and then to make offerings to the gods as part of their work. I taught them to offer sea bream they caught, kelp, rice, and the like to the gods as a custom.

Teaching 6) The heart of respect, believing, and learning

AME-NO-MIOYA-GAMI

I thought I needed to first teach the heart of respect as the starting point of my teachings in Japan. So I put my mind the most to teach the heart of respect.

I told people to have the heart of respect first. Next, I taught them to believe and then to learn. I taught them to learn and study.

Teaching 7) Order and harmony

AME-NO-MIOYA-GAMI

I taught people order and harmony like this. When God is present, of course people must proceed with things in the appropriate way to interact with God. But when God is not present, God's representatives govern the world in many cases, so people must pay respect to those who can convey God's words. And ultimately, they must respect their parents, be dutiful to them, and build a good family. I taught such things.

Japan was particularly hot and humid, and the trees were thriving, so the Japanese culture was mainly a wood culture. That's why historical traces could hardly remain. If it was a stone civilization, things could have remained more evidently, but the wood was mainly used instead of stones. I think this is why there is little evidence left to this day.

Anyway, these are what I taught.

Materials and tools Ame-no-Mioya-Gami brought from outer space

AME-NO-MIOYA-GAMI

In addition, I taught people how to make various tools. It was a civilization that mainly used wood, but I also taught people how to use a unique metallic substance. It precedes the ironware or bronzeware used today. As a precursor of modern ironware and bronzeware, I introduced a very tough stone-like substance that contains metal. We gave people such useful tools to build houses and other things, so the Japanese people in those times were using them.

It was actually a special stone. We brought a lot, and it could be used as metallic tools as well. For example, when it was attached to the end of a spear, people could use it to fight or hunt, but it could also be used to cut down trees or process things.

Because it emits a special magnetic force, it was often enshrined as an object of worship. Even now, the object of worship at the Ise Jingu Shrine may be a stone or something, but in ancient times, it was not a mere stone but a very tough ore-bearing substance that came from outer space. We brought it to Japan and had people use it. And those who were given the permission to use it basically became village chiefs.

I think it was called *hihiiro-gane*. What would it be in today's term? It was neither iron nor bronze but a substance that existed before them. It was similar to aluminum; it was light and strong. This material is often used to make flying saucers, but it is a very valuable substance on Earth. This is one of the things we gave. We also encouraged people to strive to create various things using a substitute for this stone.

By the time people were using chipped obsidian as arrowheads or spear points around Spain, metal had already been introduced to Japan. I would say that this significantly increased productivity.

We also brought certain types of animals to Japan on our spaceships, so some of them were bred only in Japan. They could be eaten as food. Some of them evolved on their own to later become animals specific to Japan.

4

The Spread of Civilization: From Japan to China and India

The Japanese civilization also influenced ancient civilizations such as Mu

B

You said you chose to descend to Japan, specifically where Mt. Fuji could be seen, 30,000 years ago. What was your purpose at that time? What was your plan in coming down to Earth, giving people the teachings, and granting them the wisdom—such as ways to make tools—to live an affluent life in this world?

AME-NO-MIOYA-GAMI

Well... Of course, we came to Earth in super ancient times and did various things, but when there was not much to do on Earth, we went to other planets. I don't think I have to talk about it too much now. It will eventually be revealed to you when it's necessary. Well, when you have much spare time, a 100-million-year history of the universe may be revealed, but I wonder who will listen to it. I don't know.

When civilizations on other planets need us, we go there. I, myself, have connections to outer space, so this galaxy is not the only place I influence. I guide other galaxies as well. I have sometimes come to watch Earth and have helped create the foundation of various civilizations. But compared to other planets in different galaxies, Earth has a unique environment, so developing civilizations that is unique to Earth is a kind of experiment.

I have been involved in different things on other planets.

B

From what you just said, I understand that you descended to Japan to create a new civilization.

AME-NO-MIOYA-GAMI

That's fine.

B

According to your plan, what kind of civilization did you intend to create in Japan?

AME-NO-MIOYA-GAMI

I emphasized creating spiritual height. The country itself was not large, but I created the origin of today's "Oriental spirit." I intended to create "Greece of the East."

You claim the Mu civilization to be at the root of the Japanese civilization, believing it's new information. But you must remember that the Mu civilization was actually influenced by the Japanese civilization. My teachings spread to the Mu continent. But the environment in Mu differed from Japan, so various things—buildings, for instance—developed differently.

Well, compared to me, Ra Mu is a much younger soul. I'm guessing that's the limit of your understanding. I am a being that is not supposed to descend to earth so easily.

SHIO OKAWA

Japanese school textbooks state that the teachings of respect and order, which you mentioned earlier, are Confucian values that were introduced to Japan from China and the Korean Peninsula. They also say the culture of using bronzeware and ironware came from those countries. But now I understand very well that these things were taught or brought to Japan by Lord Ame-no-Mioya-Gami 30,000 years ago.

AME-NO-MIOYA-GAMI

Yes.

SHIO OKAWA

As I listen to you, I thought your teachings contain elements similar to the teachings of Confucius, so I assume you had a significant influence on Chinese culture as well. In China, there is a being called "Tiandi," or the Emperor of Heaven. What's your connection to Tiandi?

AME-NO-MIOYA-GAMI

Hmm... I think India is older than China as a civilization. China thinks they have a history of 4,000 to 5,000 years, right? But the Indian civilization is much older. I think Vishnu[5] appeared in India after my time. Vishnu appeared and led India. There was the civilization of India created by Vishnu. However, Southwest Asia down to Egypt area was still largely

The picture of Vishnu on Garuda's back.

affected by other gods, so various things flowed into India because of its location.

Then, the civilization spread from India to China. It went from India to China, causing another civilization to rise in China about several thousand years ago. China created the height of civilization about 2,000 or 3,000 years before Confucius' time—that's about 5,000 years ago from now. Because it was a continent, China had plenty of people and crops, so a civilization was created to a certain degree. But before that, the civilization was introduced from India.

And actually, the Indian civilization was introduced from Japan. So the civilization spread from Japan to India, from India to China, then back to Japan via the Korean Peninsula. Such a cycle exists. On one part, the Japanese civilization

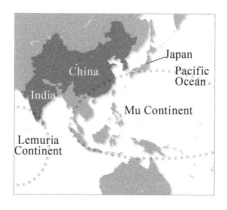

spread to India, but on another part, it also spread to the Mu continent.

From the perspective of world history, Japan's position is much like that of ancient Greece, or it is similar to Jewish history in the context of Christian civilization. Those are what the Japanese civilization can be compared to.

The reason the Japanese archipelago was separated from the continent

A

So what is your spiritual connection to Vishnu or Tiandi of China?

AME-NO-MIOYA-GAMI

Hmm. They may be some portion of me.

A

Portion? So are they, at the very least, a part of you?

AME-NO-MIOYA-GAMI

They are "domestic," aren't they? I'm managing several planets in other galaxies of the universe. So I have a bigger mission.

A

The civilization spread to India, China, Mu, and even as far as Africa, so there are quite a lot of things that have branched from you. Is that right?

AME-NO-MIOYA-GAMI

Yes, that's right. But the level of the material development of each civilization is greatly affected by climate, and a country's land and population. I have concurrently been carrying out experiments on various civilizations in different places, but I have to admit there are differences. So I have guided them according to their speed of development.

In the case of Earth, it has been affected by truly many different planets, so sometimes various things were mixed in. There weren't any problems when it was aiming to improve, but there were times when it regressed, and wars broke out frequently. So I often came (to Earth) when I had to rebuild it.

The reason I thought to separate the Japanese archipelago from the Eurasian continent—where Russia and China are— was because there were many ferocious races over there. They would come into Japan in large numbers if the lands were connected, so that's why I thought it had to be separated and did so.

A

"Ame-no-Mioya-Gami" is the name you were called when you lived in Japan, but is there any other name of yours that remains in other countries?

AME-NO-MIOYA-GAMI

If you call "GOD," expressed in bold capital letters, it would mean me.

A

So you are the existence of such a big scale.

AME-NO-MIOYA-GAMI

Yes. I am not only in charge of Earth. I only come here occasionally when I have things to do.

5

The Relationship between Ame-no-Mioya-Gami and El Cantare

The difference between the God of the Universe and the God of the Earth

A

What I didn't quite understand from the last spiritual message was the relationship between you and El Cantare. There might be some secret regarding this. The fact that you suddenly came to Earth from outer space 30,000 years ago must mean there was some reason.

AME-NO-MIOYA-GAMI

Well, how can I put it? You say El Cantare has branch spirits[6] who were born on earth once every 2,000 or 3,000 years over the past 10,000 years or more, or from the time of Ra Mu, right?

A

Yes.

AME-NO-MIOYA-GAMI

Other than that, you also say there are beings like Alpha[7], Elohim[8], and El Cantare who are the Lord of all gods. But I'm saying there is still another part of him above these.

A

Above them?

AME-NO-MIOYA-GAMI

Yes. There is another part above a being called El Cantare. You call El Cantare the God of the Earth, don't you?

A

Yes.

AME-NO-MIOYA-GAMI

There is another part above the God of the Earth—the God of the Universe.

A

The God of the Universe...

AME-NO-MIOYA-GAMI

Yes. There is another part—the God of the Universe—on a higher level above El Cantare, that is guiding some "Messiah

Planets"—the most advanced planets in different galaxies of the universe. There is such a connection.

A

Within that structure, is it you who unites all these planets?

AME-NO-MIOYA-GAMI

Well, the universe is too large to be united.

A

It is too large.

AME-NO-MIOYA-GAMI

It is too large to do so. I am mainly involved in the groups of planets and galaxies that influence Earth. But since I cannot unite all of them by myself, I share the responsibilities with others.

The Messiah Planets exist in other galaxies as well. So, there are other beings who are in charge of those places but have yet to influence Earth. This is beyond your understanding, though.

A

Is it correct to assume you were based in Andromeda before coming to Earth?

AME-NO-MIOYA-GAMI

Well, that was not the only place.

A

It wasn't the only place?

AME-NO-MIOYA-GAMI

No, it was not the only place. There was more than one. I was supervising at least five planets at the same time.

A

Which planets were they, for example?

AME-NO-MIOYA-GAMI

Andromeda is one of them, but there were other constellations that have a significant influence on Earth. I traveled to such constellations on occasion.

Andromeda is relatively far away. The reason I was based in Andromeda was... hmm... Well, some beings who intended to destroy Earth had come to Andromeda, so I went to gain a foothold there as well.

There are Messiahs on other planets as well

AME-NO-MIOYA-GAMI

Hmm... Well, the universe is vast. Just counting the number of galaxies, it is believed there are more than 100 billion. So unfortunately, it is difficult. (Note: According to an investigation by NASA, it is estimated that there are about two trillion galaxies within the observable universe.)

A

Hmm...

AME-NO-MIOYA-GAMI

You already know some galaxies from your "space people reading"—the galaxies containing the home planets of the souls you have investigated. I am often involved with the various Messiah Planets—planets where Messiahs live—in those galaxies. Of course, they call me by a different name in those places.

A

I see.

SHIO OKAWA

Am I correct in assuming that the beings called "Messiahs" are connected to the Primordial God of the universe or the Primordial Buddha?

AME-NO-MIOYA-GAMI

Hmm... [*About five seconds of silence.*] Well, Messiahs are like the general manager of a hotel. So there is the general manager of "Hotel Earth," and there are general managers on other planets. Many galaxies exist, and each galaxy has many general managers. There are leaders among them. So, there are several "General Messiahs of messiahs" in each galaxy. And the general leaders of certain galaxies gather to organize yet another assembly of senior Messiahs.

The universe is much bigger than you imagine. It is much, much bigger.

"I'm a national of the universe"

A

In your last spiritual message, you mentioned the number "11" as in the "11th dimension." Are we correct in understanding that you are from the 11th dimension?

AME-NO-MIOYA-GAMI

If I were to put it in a way you can understand, perhaps I am from that dimension.

Listen, the universe that appears in Vishnu's dream is like a drop of water; many universes are floating like drops of water in his dream. Galaxies are born and disappear while Vishnu takes a nap. That's how the galaxies are. And this Vishnu is only one portion of me.

A

Your portion.

AME-NO-MIOYA-GAMI

Yes. So I'm much bigger.

Hmm... You're saying something like... You bring up different names like Alpha, Elohim, Ra Mu, Thoth, and...

A

Rient Arl Croud and...

AME-NO-MIOYA-GAMI

Those are the rulers of a continent, right? They are like the rulers of a continent. But I am not necessarily a national of Earth. I have the name "Ame-no-Mioya-Gami," and my nationality is the universe, so... how can I put it? Both Alpha and Elohim are "nationals of Earth." Am I right?

SHIO OKAWA

But your soul is connected to El Cantare, isn't it?

AME-NO-MIOYA-GAMI

Yes, I think so. Probably, yes.

How can I explain it? [*Pointing at the pattern of the halo in the prayer room*.] Look at this strange mandala-like pattern here. It is not as easy to understand me as pointing at a specific part of the pattern and saying, "I'm this part." There are different levels, and together they make a whole. You see the mandala has many different patterns. In the middle, there are one, two, three, four, five, six, seven... eight petals, and there is a central point inside. There are eight petals, and then there are additional petals and many lotus flower-like patterns around it. We are just like this mandala in reality. We are divided into many layers of light and are illuminating the universe.

It is extremely difficult to say how many mandalas like this exist. As long as you are human, you are not allowed to know the answer. If you ask me which position I assume in this mandala... Can you see the eight petals surrounding the central point? I think I am one of those petals.

SHIO OKAWA

In that case, are we correct in assuming you are fairly close to the core consciousness and are shedding light on a wide area of the universe?

AME-NO-MIOYA-GAMI

Hmm... Well, my consciousness is actually much larger.

As a matter of fact, I don't have much to do on Earth. I normally don't have things to do here, but should doomsday approach Earth, I have to come and do my work. I would have to decide where you should immigrate to. So, at that time, I would have to come back again. But other than that, I usually don't have so many things to do. I just leave it to those who specialize in Earth to take care of things on Earth.

You should know that the Original God of Japan is quite a great being.

6

The Reason Why a Highly Advanced Civilization Was Established in Japan

A large-scale nuclear war occurred 30,000 years ago

A

As for the earlier question about the reason you came to Earth...

AME-NO-MIOYA-GAMI

What's wrong with me coming here?

A

Of course, there is nothing wrong...

AME-NO-MIOYA-GAMI

Huh?

B

We feel very honored.

AME-NO-MIOYA-GAMI

Hm.

A

I thought there might actually be a bigger secret behind the reason why you came to Earth 30,000 years ago.

AME-NO-MIOYA-GAMI

Hmm... Well, there was a major war around that time. It was an extremely large-scale war. It was something similar to a nuclear war.

A

Really.

AME-NO-MIOYA-GAMI

Such a war occurred. It was exactly as it is described in the Indian epic poetry. There was once a crisis of Earth possibly being destroyed by a nuclear war.

A

Is that so?

AME-NO-MIOYA-GAMI

So the civilization escaped and moved from the current Eurasian continent toward Mu, Lemuria, and Atlantis. The Eurasian continent underwent a massive upheaval because it was experiencing something like radioactive contamination for some time.

A

So that's what happened.

AME-NO-MIOYA-GAMI

It was a huge collapse of a civilization. For the people living in the area, it was as if they were experiencing something like doomsday. So, the civilization moved to other continents. That's why I thought it was necessary to create a spiritual civilization in Japan, which was the closest to Eurasia. Things have calmed down again and now, the Eurasian continent expands with much power in the modern civilization.

So there was something like a major nuclear war centering around India before I came to Earth. After that, another major war, which was also similar to a nuclear war, occurred in the American continent, too. Well, these things cannot be helped. If the damage does not spread to a global scale, we simply move the civilization to other continents and have people start all over there. And when things calm down, and nature returns to its original state, we build a civilization once again in those damaged areas.

But it was terrible back then. Large areas of land turned into deserts as a result.

A

Oh...

AME-NO-MIOYA-GAMI

Many deserts formed across quite a large area—from the deserts in Southwest Asia to the Gobi Desert. Civilizations completely collapsed in those areas—they were all swept away.

A

I see. That's what happened.

AME-NO-MIOYA-GAMI

There was an extremely large-scale war.

The height of the East was maintained in Japan

A

It seems to me that the gods related to Japanese Shinto must have had a much more important role after your descent to Japan.

AME-NO-MIOYA-GAMI

For the time being, they had to keep the quality of the civilization at a certain level, even if it was not on a large scale. That was one of their goals.

You probably learn at school that Japan was civilized when kanji characters were introduced around the sixth century, and you are brainwashed to believe such a history. But it is all nonsense. It is all wrong. The height of the East was maintained in Japan, and Japan had the function of "exporting" civilizations to other continents as the need arose.

I, myself, am technically an alien, but I tried my best to look like an earthling in appearance. I might have looked like the great statue of Nio (guardian deity of Buddha) [*laughs*] because I was rather big. But I had to show that God has dignity and teach people that there is a Being above humans. Otherwise, humans won't be humble. They won't be humble and won't be able to create a society where people help each other, cooperate with each other, and trust each other. That's why I thought God was necessary, and I created gods in the Earth's Spirit World. But it is also a fact that space people occasionally came to Earth in physical bodies to raise the awareness of the earthlings; these beings called themselves "gods."

Even so, this doesn't mean I suddenly came to have a connection to Earth. I have been involved with Earth's affairs since very ancient times when the plan was first made to have humans live on Earth. Well, I was certainly discussing things with Mr. El Miore.

A

Is that so?

AME-NO-MIOYA-GAMI

Yes, Mr. El Miore—Mr. El Miore who was working hard on Venus just recently.

A

I see.

AME-NO-MIOYA-GAMI

I think he has primary responsibility for Earth. I am an advisor, so I didn't have primary responsibility. I just came to advise Mr. El Miore so he could do well on Earth.

Ame-no-Mioya-Gami's connection to Amaterasu-O-Mikami and other gods

B

I understand that the great origin or a great current of the Japanese civilization was established ever since you descended to Japan. The gods of Japanese Shinto appeared within this great current, and the names of Amaterasu-O-Mikami—the leading deity of Japan—and other gods have been revealed. Would you tell us about your relation to these gods?

AME-NO-MIOYA-GAMI

Amaterasu was originally on Vega. I think Mr. El Cantare issued a "personnel change" and called her to come to Earth. At that time, He probably considered where to position her. That was how it went.

SHIO OKAWA

Does this mean Lord El Cantare is in a position to issue "personnel changes," including those in Vega?

AME-NO-MIOYA-GAMI

Yes, of course, he is. I think he watches over all the planets that have a direct connection to Earth as a group, much like "Happy Science Group."

SHIO OKAWA

Like a CEO [*laughs*].

The true nature of the Supreme God-like Beings in Vega and Pleiades

B

The space people readings we conducted in the past have revealed there are also Supreme God-like Beings—the same existence as El Cantare—on other planets such as Vega and Pleiades, which are said to have a deep connection to Earth. But their names and teachings have yet to be revealed to us. May I ask you to reveal a little more about them?

AME-NO-MIOYA-GAMI

They are the same being. Mr. El Miore became Mr. El Cantare. It was just that before becoming what he is, Mr. El Cantare was on various planets, including Vega and Pleiades, and called himself by a different name appropriate for each planet. They are the same being.

B

What was the name of the Lord in Vega or Pleiades if you were to express it in the Earth's modern language?

AME-NO-MIOYA-GAMI

Well, if you think of some possible names between El Miore and El Cantare, it's probably something like that. Yes, I could give him a name if you want. How about "El Vegan"? Hahaha [*laughs*]. El Vegan sounds good, doesn't it? Or how about "El Pleidest"? (Note: After this spiritual message, "The Spiritual Message from Heem—The Leading God of Vega" was recorded on November 12, 2018. This spiritual message revealed that the ruling God of Vega is called Heem and is the Supreme God-like Being connected to the core consciousness of El Cantare.)

A

[*Laughs*] I see. Thank you very much.

7

Secrets of the Universe, As Stated by Ame-no-Mioya-Gami

There is no beginning or end to the time of the universe

A

Could you please teach us the profound truth about the beginning of the universe as you perceive it?

AME-NO-MIOYA-GAMI

You (Happy Science) teach that the universe has a history of 100 billion years, but to me, 100 billion years ago happened just recently.

A

Oh, really.

AME-NO-MIOYA-GAMI

I think it's pointless to tell humans such a small-scale story for children.

The flow of time in the universe is like Yamanote Loop Line in Tokyo; it goes round and round without beginning or end. You might say Tokyo Station is the starting station, but it is also the last station on the line. So time exists, but at the same time, it doesn't exist. In truth, time circulates within the universe.

Because time circulates endlessly, you cannot cut it at the 100-billion-year mark. It's not something you can cut. If you think you can cut time at a certain point, it means you think of time as something like the Tokaido Shinkansen Line that stretches in a linear manner rather than in a loop like the Yamanote Line. That's how you perceive time. You think time is something that only moves forward in a straight line like a flying arrow.

The space civilization will begin within the stream of the El Cantare civilization

A

Then, how will the age of the universe unfold on Earth in the future?

AME-NO-MIOYA-GAMI

I think it will be very interesting in 100 years.

A

Interesting?

AME-NO-MIOYA-GAMI

Yes, it will be interesting because you will finally catch up to the level of other space people in the universe. You will catch up very soon. Then, the "lid" covering the unknown information up until now will be opened. You'll be invited to other planets, and you will be able to travel back and forth between other planets and Earth. Those from other planets will also appear, and there will be a greater exchange between Earth and other planets. Like how New York today has developed with the influx of people from different countries, a time will soon come when you and other space people visit each other.

You need to make further efforts to make it happen. You need to try harder. But I think such a time is just around the corner.

Now that El Cantare is born on earth, the space civilization will surely begin within the stream of the El Cantare civilization. Of course, you have to work harder, but these teachings will probably guide you into the space civilization. I don't know whether the "envoys on ships" will come from other planets or you will send the "envoys on ships" to their planets, but the exchange of civilizations will soon take place. I don't think it will be long before it happens.

So you must aim to be a world religion. Christianity and Islam are becoming a thing of the past. And so are Buddhism and Confucianism. I think they will be incorporated into Happy Science. I don't know whether you call it "El Cantare-ism" or "Happy Science-ism," but what you are teaching will be the central ideas of Earth, and people will have to make them the backbone of Earth when interacting with those from other planets.

After all, it is necessary to demonstrate the level of development of a planet's civilization. You have to show how far you have advanced into the universe when negotiating with the Messiahs of other planets. If it's possible to interact, an exchange between civilizations will likely begin.

Your Messiah has certain connections to different planets and galaxies, so it may be difficult to understand his position in the entire universe. I think his power isn't so weak in regard to his awareness. The universe is too vast to understand everything in it, but at least he has some authority over the space you can observe through a telescope.

Is it possible to understand
the Primordial Buddha of the entire universe?

A

There are Messiahs of the universe and General Messiahs, but above them are yet other superior Messiahs. Is the so-called the Primordial Buddha...

AME-NO-MIOYA-GAMI

Ah, are you trying to understand such a being?

A

Yes.

AME-NO-MIOYA-GAMI

Are you trying to have me explain that far? Then, I would have to talk about the 20th dimension or above.

A

If you could tell us in a way we would understand...

AME-NO-MIOYA-GAMI

You'd better give up on it.

A

We have to give up on it... [*smiles wryly*].

AME-NO-MIOYA-GAMI

It is like ascending in a glass elevator and looking down at the city's night view. So you simply need to elevate your point of view.

A

Do you recognize that Being?

AME-NO-MIOYA-GAMI

Huh? No way. There's no way I can know everything.

A

Oh, I see.

AME-NO-MIOYA-GAMI

Of course, I don't. That's why I say "*Mr.* El Cantare." It means I am on equal footing.

A

But according to the teaching we have learned, El Cantare is equal to the Primordial Buddha.

AME-NO-MIOYA-GAMI

Yes, that is *your* Primordial Buddha. But it is difficult to know where you are situated in the entire universe. Maybe you'd better pray there is no universe more advanced than yours.

The flip-side universe is like a sewage system

A

If I may ask, how do you recognize the flip-side universe?

AME-NO-MIOYA-GAMI

Oh, it's just like sewage, so you don't have to worry about that.

A

Sewage?

AME-NO-MIOYA-GAMI

It is a "sewage system." It is always necessary, so it can't be helped.

A

I see. You mean it is not comparable to the front-side universe in size.

AME-NO-MIOYA-GAMI

Urban life would not be possible without a sewage system. Without it, sewage would overflow on the ground and give off a terrible smell; it would cause a lot of trouble. That's why the sewage network runs underground while railways and metropolitan expressways run above ground.

How Ame-no-Mioya-Gami understands the parallel world

A

Let me ask you another question. How do you understand the parallel world?

AME-NO-MIOYA-GAMI

I wonder if you really believe you can understand it using weak words like "parallel world." You know, you yourselves are living in at least two worlds now.

A

We are?

AME-NO-MIOYA-GAMI

Yes. You sleep about eight hours a day, don't you? The world you go to while sleeping isn't the world you are now living in, is it?

A

It's the Spirit World.

AME-NO-MIOYA-GAMI

You go to a different world, right?

A

Right.

AME-NO-MIOYA-GAMI

While sleeping, people sometimes go to the Spirit World and explore mainly the areas they live in and come back, but those with a higher spiritual ability will go to the spiritual realms beyond that. They can travel to both the past and the future and can also transcend space. Some people have such experiences. This is technically the parallel world as well.

But if you think the parallel world is somewhere on the opposite side of the world, which is exactly like yours—where there is the same flow of time, and the same people, including you, live—then it is a bit different. It isn't easy to clarify the true secrets of the Spirit World while having a physical body. It is difficult to understand.

If you enter the parallel world in your current condition, you will likely be taken to a mental hospital. It is impossible to have such a level of awareness. If you want to enter the parallel world in the truest sense in the daytime while you are awake, you would have to travel at a speed that exceeds the speed of light. It is a world you can see when you exceed the speed of light.

Master Ryuho will teach it if he wants to, but he may not if he doesn't want to. There must be a proper time for him to reveal it. This is something god Vishnu knows well, too. In any case, such a time will eventually come. But you are still at a level where you have to memorize English words as a second language, so perhaps it's better not to think about such complex matters.

A

I understand.

8

The Power of the Universe at the Root of the Japanese People

The healing power described in the movie, *Immortal Hero*

B

We are nearing the end of our session.

AME-NO-MIOYA-GAMI

Right.

B

I think the video of this spiritual message will be shown to people before the release of our movie, *Immortal Hero*. The main character of this movie is named Makoto Mioya. Were you the one who gave us the inspiration about the main character's name?

AME-NO-MIOYA-GAMI

Well, I thought I would let you use my name.

B

What message should we convey to those who watch this movie?

AME-NO-MIOYA-GAMI

Oh, I forgot to tell you this earlier, but one of the reasons people had faith in me when I was called Ame-no-Mioya-Gami was my healing power. People came to worship me because my power to cure various illnesses was very strong. How do I put it? Well, it was not exactly a radioactive ray, but in a sense, it was one of the powers of the universe. Many illnesses on Earth could be cured by being exposed to that power.

Another reason I could cure illnesses is connected to the axis of time, which I mentioned earlier. I could "turn back time" as if rebooting a system, and make people return to a healthy state. I could even make sick people return to a healthy state. Once they returned to their original state, their bodily functions were renewed.

So using the rays of the universe or something like the radioactive rays of the universe, which are unknown to you, was one way to cure people's illnesses. And the other way was to get people to go back to a time when the cause of the illness had occurred. Usually, there is a reason for illnesses to occur, and as a result, the cause manifests itself as an illness. So I have the sick person replace the mind that has been causing the illness with the right mind. Then, the illness that resulted from the cause becomes cured, and various parts of the body get renewed. For this reason, one's life span is almost non-existent.

The mechanism for life experiences to continue eternally

AME-NO-MIOYA-GAMI

This is already well-known in Japanese myths. The Japanese myth, "Urashima Taro," talks about how the protagonist, Taro spends three years in Ryugu-jo (the Dragon Palace) under the sea to find out later that he was gone for 300 years. The same is true for the stories of "Umisachi Yamasachi"; there is a similar story of years passing while the sea god's daughter was entertaining Yamasachi.

When traveling through space at a speed that exceeds the speed of light, you need to be very good at setting the time you want to come back; otherwise, you will go too far into the future or too far into the past.

I used the analogy of the Yamanote Line, but the truth is, the "train schedule" is much busier; if I compare the Yamanote Line to a ring of time, there are many layers of such loop lines running in the universe. Those inside the ring of time cannot get out of it, but if there is anyone who can teleport to a neighboring loop, he or she can move to another time and space. This is similar to being in a parallel world; once you move to a different time and space, you will be in a different flow of time.

In other words, the universe is designed for humans to continue having life experiences eternally. There is a flow of history consisting of series of events, and as long as you are "on that Yamanote Line," each event will happen in a set order, much like how regular trains stop at each station in order. But if you could jump aboard "another Yamanote Line" that is intersecting yours, you would experience the history of "another humanity" from its beginning to end.

In fact, the loop lines overlap in multiple layers. So the parallel world is not about the two worlds running in parallel; the different rings of time and space run through the universe in multiple layers. Neither Einstein nor Hawking could see or understand this, but your Master probably knows. So maybe the time will come when he can teach this. I am also someone who uses this system.

So, the past, the present, and the future are all at a single point. Earth, Vega, Pleiades, Andromeda, and other planets are like stations you automatically arrive at while riding on the loop train. If you miss your station, it will come around again an hour later. So we are traveling through space in that way. This is how it works.

I am in a position to make sure all the lines are running smoothly. Well, that's who I am. But I also need a break, so I have others to fill in for me when I take time off. I have a few people like that. That is how you can understand me.

The Japanese civilization has a much longer history than 2,000 years

AME-NO-MIOYA-GAMI

It is difficult to tell you my relation to Mr. El Miore, Mr. El Cantare, Mr. Alpha, and Mr. Elohim. At the very least, I cannot make my appearance as long as the Japanese civilization is "shortened" to this extent and is considered having a history of less than 2,000 years; all I can say would be, "I am Japan's leading God who lives in the parallel world."

I expect this spiritual message will reveal my "face" just a little. But it would only be as though people see me passing on the train on the opposite track and wonder, "Who was it that I saw out the window just now?"

I used the title "Mr." but this doesn't mean they are in a lower position. We are just working on different missions now. We have the same nature. We are actually the same, the same person. Well, we are not people but the same God or the same Buddha—I don't know how to put it exactly, but it's something like that.

SHIO OKAWA

But you are the main God of Japanese Shinto or at its root. This is the truth I really want the Japanese people to know.

AME-NO-MIOYA-GAMI

That's right.

SHIO OKAWA

I hope as many people as possible will watch our movie and come to know that such a great God is at the top of Japanese Shinto.

AME-NO-MIOYA-GAMI

Yes. Mr. Thoth is now guiding Mr. Trump. He is guiding the world through Mr. Trump, so I think he is trying to work with him.

Is this the second time for the soul of El Cantare to be involved in the Japanese civilization?

SHIO OKAWA

There is one last point I'd like to ask. Since the start of Happy Science, we have learned that the soul of Master Ryuho Okawa was born in Japan for the first time. We think you have made your appearance this time because the range of our teachings has been expanding. In this sense, are we correct in assuming that this is the second time Master's soul was involved in the Japanese civilization?

AME-NO-MIOYA-GAMI

Well, I descended from the sky, so I was not born Japanese. But I landed in Japan, so in that sense, I am Japanese. Well, I am multinational. Or I could say I have "dual citizenship." This is true of other gods as well. The gods of the sky that appeared in the past all have dual citizenship.

Ancient people couldn't tell "gods" from "space people." They could be the same, but they are not always the same. Some descended to Kyushu in southern Japan. Some descended to the area around Nara Prefecture. And others descended to the area near Mt. Fuji. They landed in various places.

What I want to say is, Japan is by no means inferior to the countries such as Judea, India, China, and European countries. I want people to know this. You say that people escaped from Mu (to Japan). While this is true, I want you to know it was Japan that had influenced Mu as well.

But this is just a recent event. It happened only tens of thousands of years ago, so the events that happened over hundreds of millions of years ago are yet another story. There are many other stories. If you want to confirm what I am saying, ask Mr. Alpha, Mr. Elohim, or others like them. But I am not sure how accurate they will be; it depends on whether they recognized Japan or not.

At any rate, I am the one who appeared with a physical body and was worshiped as God. It's unfortunate how nothing is left now because my palace was made of wood. Today, there are many religious groups at the foot of Mt. Fuji. There seems to be a magnetic field that attracts them there. Eventually, you, too, may have to do something.

Well, when I arrived initially, Mt. Fuji had just started to erupt. I came to stop the eruption.

A

Did you stop the eruption?

AME-NO-MIOYA-GAMI

Yes, I did. I stopped the eruption. I stopped it at that time and let the trees grow. I was the one who came here to stop it.

Rescue on the space level might come when Earth is in crisis

B

This will be my last question. I think the fact that you have spiritually come down now means Japan is standing at the crucial crossroads again. What kind of mindset should we Japanese people have from now on?

AME-NO-MIOYA-GAMI

Well, it is not really the crossroads. You have to be the pilots or the navigators. You have a mission as the navigators of the Earth civilization. It is as if you are standing on the bow of a ship and watching ahead. Because you have such a mission, you have to predict or indicate the fate of the Earth civilization. The exchange with the space civilization will begin next, so now, you need to make preparations to reach that stage.

Several crises are scheduled to occur on Earth, so the question is how to overcome them. How will El Cantare and his disciples get through the 21st century? I have to watch how this goes. It is my work to come to the rescue on the space level if the worst happens. I do not intend to intervene directly, but I will intervene when you need salvation on the space level.

You seem to be very scared of reptilians and the like, but to me, they are nothing; they can all be wiped out with a single spray of "pesticide." So you can come to me for help when the worst happens.

I want you to call to the Japanese people so they can regain even a fragment of faith. I am sure Amaterasu will do her best, too. Mr. El Cantare is working hard, so I think he will do something. He understands the multidimensional parallel world in the multidimensional universe, which I mentioned earlier, and has grasped it as part of his enlightenment. So I think he will teach about it if it's necessary.

A

All right. Thank you very much for today.

AME-NO-MIOYA-GAMI

[*To Shio Okawa.*] Shouldn't I tell you what you looked like?

A

Then, please.

AME-NO-MIOYA-GAMI

She was a beautiful woman.

A

Did she come down with you?

AME-NO-MIOYA-GAMI

No, she didn't. She is an Earth-born soul, so she didn't. She was created from inside the soul of El Miore, or El Cantare, so she is different from other human species. She was specially created as God's divided soul.

A

Thank you very much for today.

AME-NO-MIOYA-GAMI

OK.

9

There Is Still Much More to the Teachings of Ame-no-Mioya-Gami

RYUHO OKAWA

[*Claps hands three times.*] He was unique.

A

[*Laughs.*]

RYUHO OKAWA

I think he didn't speak Japanese in the previous session (Chapter One) because he wasn't willing to answer Interviewer A's questions. He probably didn't want to, because conversations with Interviewer A could end up sounding too comical. But it is also likely true that he was involved in other work.

A

I see. That makes sense.

RYUHO OKAWA

Maybe he cannot say much unless our teachings spread further and people are more prepared to listen to what we have to say.

It will be easier for him to speak if people realize that what we are saying makes more sense than what is said by Hawking or Einstein. But there is a low-level aspect in Japan's "media democracy," so the truth may be left unsaid unless religions regain the true respect of people.

To me, he seems to have more in reserve; it seems there is still much more to his teachings.

That's all for today.

ALL INTERVIEWERS

Thank you very much.

EDITOR'S NOTES

1 Takenouchi-no-Sukune

The great grandchild of the eighth emperor of Japan, Kogen. Many legendary stories remain about him, such as he served as the minister for five consecutive emperors, helped Empress Jingu when she sent troops to Silla (one of the three kingdoms of Korea), and lived until 300 years old.

2 Thoth

See the end section.

3 Ra Mu

See the end section.

4 Vega

The first magnitude-star in the constellation Lyra. Vegans can transform themselves according to the other person's wish. They have three genders: male, female, and neuter. They have highly advanced scientific technologies and healing power.

5 Vishnu

The god of Hinduism. In one of the Brahmanas, *Rigveda*, he was called the God of the Sun and later became one of the highest gods along with Brahma and Shiva. It is said that he maintains the universe. He has 10 avatars to save the people, and some of which are Rama, Krishna, and Buddha.

6 El Cantare's branch spirits

See the end section.

7 Alpha

See the end section.

8 Elohim

See the end section.

Afterword

This book has a different nature from the Laws I have taught so far.

Ame-no-Mioya-Gami says that he had come down to the foothills of Mt. Fuji from the Andromeda Galaxy about 30,000 years ago, with a huge fleet of roughly 200,000 people.

I'm sure further details will soon be revealed. This book tells that Japan's Great God had existed more than 27,000 years before Emperor Jimmu's military expedition to the east. However, given that the "Laws of El Cantare" teaches the appearance of the Original God Alpha 330 million years ago, it is nothing to be surprised about.

By reading this book, Japanese people will truly feel proud to have been born in Japan. Also, the readers will be able to understand why the "Laws of El Cantare" have been dispatched from this country.

This may not be the kind of book that should be sold to the general public in bookstores. To those who got a hold of this book even by chance, I hope you treat it as a precious piece.

Ryuho Okawa
Master & CEO of Happy Science Group
January 13, 2019

PART TWO

The Lecture on *The Descent of Ame-no-Mioya-Gami*

Preface

This is truly a mysterious story. The Japanese civilization is commonly believed to have a history of about 3,000 years, but this book claims that the descent of Ame-no-Mioya-Gami took place about 30,000 years ago. Apparently, Ame-no-Mioya-Gami had come from the Andromeda Galaxy with about 200,000 people on spaceships and descended on the wilderness on the Shizuoka Prefecture side where you can see Mt. Fuji. What events took place in the next 27,000 years? The gods described in *Kojiki* (Records of Ancient Matters) and *Nihon Shoki* (Chronicles of Japan) made their appearance, and Emperor Jimmu made the military expedition to the east.

This blank time in history needs to be filled. The teachings of Ame-no-Mioya-Gami cover manners, the heart of respect, and the way of harmony. So, there is no doubt that he is at the origin of Japanese Shinto.

Although these are not compiled in this book, there are other spiritual messages which said that the "God" revered by the legendary holy kings of ancient China—

Yao and Shun—is the same being as Ame-no-Mioya-Gami. Shun married the two daughters of Yao, and one of them—Nuying—is assumed to be Doutei-ko nyan-nyan (the goddess Lake Dongting). This is probably why she calls herself a disciple of El Cantare.

Ryuho Okawa
Master & CEO of Happy Science Group
February 2, 2021

CHAPTER ONE

The Lecture on *The Descent of Ame-no-Mioya-Gami*

The Origin of the Japanese Civilization

Originally recorded in Japanese on February 5, 2019
at General Headquarters, Happy Science, Japan
and later translated into English.

1

Ame-no-Mioya-Gami that Appears in
Hotsuma Tsutae

Differences between *Kojiki* and *Nihon Shoki*, which were compiled around the same time

This is the lecture on Part One of this book. If you read it, you can probably understand what is being written. All I can say is, "It's just as it's written." Since it may be difficult for my disciples to lecture on it, I would be happy to add some points to help you deepen your understanding on this occasion.

In terms of its content, there are still many unclear aspects. I myself have not contacted Ame-no-Mioya-Gami so often either. But I will try to make some additional points.

The first Japanese history books are *Kojiki* and *Nihon Shoki*. *Kojiki* was compiled in AD 712 and *Nihon Shoki* in AD 720. They are eight years apart, but their contents are very different. *Kojiki* contains many mythological stories, whereas *Nihon Shoki* contains less and has more about the history of emperors. In terms of quantity, *Nihon Shoki* has more volumes. Ame-no-Mioya-Gami appears in neither of these books.

In *Kojiki*, a god called Ame-no-Minakanushi-no-Kami appears first. There also appear other gods that do not have a physical body called "hitori-gami"—meaning gods who do not marry and have no family. *Kojiki* begins with the stories of such gods and describes the appearance of many other gods, and then it shifts to describing more about people related to the imperial family. On the other hand, *Nihon Shoki* starts with the appearance of Kuni-no-Tokotachi-no-Kami and so on. Amaterasu-O-Mikami appears in *Kojiki*, but in *Nihon Shoki*, I think she appears under the name, Ohirume-no-Muchi.

Hotsuma Tsutae is written in hotsuma characters and refers to Ame-no-Mioya-Gami

Although this is not considered an official history book, there is yet an older document called *Hotsuma Tsutae*. It is considered unofficial, so it may be difficult to decide how to view the book. It is written in a unique writing system called "hotsuma characters." Given that such characters are used to write *Hotsuma Tsutae*, it should generally be regarded as an old document.

It would be a different story if there were someone during the Edo period (1603–1868) or the era before that who was so talented in language that he could invent hotsuma characters to write about the history of the imperial family. Just like how medieval Latin and other languages were born, it's possible to hypothesize that a person could invent a constructed language like Latin or Sanskrit of ancient India and wrote the ancient stories. But the timeline is quite unclear, which is typical of Japanese documents.

One of the writings of the founder of Tenrikyo Miki Nakayama is *Doroumi Koki* ("Ancient Records of the Muddy Waters"). It introduces a story of super ancient times of over 900 million years ago. The story starts with a turtle crawling in a muddy ocean like the Ariake sea. It is probably a sort of "Genesis" for them. She wrote such a story.

It is said that *Hotsuma Tsutae* was written by Takenouchi-no-Sukune. His name itself is well-known. I think it was before World War II, but in those times, a Japanese bill had the portrait of Takenouchi-no-Sukune with a long beard, though it was most probably an imaginary picture. I don't know how the picture was drawn—whether someone spiritually saw him or just imagined him, but he was most likely well-known before World War II.

If I were to raise a difference from *Kojiki* and *Nihon Shoki*, the name Ame-no-Mioya-Gami appears in *Hotsuma Tsutae* as the God that existed before Ame-no-Minakanushi-no-Kami.

I'm not sure how to pronounce the kanji characters for Ame-no-Mioya-Gami exactly; it could be Ame-no-Mioya-Kami or Ame-no-Mioya-no-Kami, but I decided to call Ame-no-Mioya-Gami because I find it easy to pronounce. If *Hotsuma Tsutae* is approved, Ame-no-Mioya-Gami is the oldest God that appears.

Ame-no-Mioya-Gami came down from the universe with a large fleet about 30,000 years ago

Other than *Hotsuma Tsutae*, the story of ancient Japanese history appears in our spiritual messages as well, including one from Ohirume-no-Muchi. According to the spiritual message from Ohirume-no-Muchi, the Japanese archipelago started to separate from the continent about 200,000 to 300,000 years ago. It became an independent island country, away from China and Russia. It had its original culture, but about 30,000 years ago, some beings came from the universe in a large fleet. This kind of story can be found in other parts of the world as well, and I think it is a possible story.

Even a history of 30,000 years is short. I am talking about the history of 300 million years. Thirty thousand years to 300 million is about 10,000 times apart, so I don't know how many times space beings had landed on Earth. But anyway, Ame-no-Mioya-Gami says he came from the Andromeda Galaxy about 30,000 years ago with about 200,000 people, which suggests that a very large number of spaceships had come. And he says he landed on a place where Mt. Fuji could be seen now—the area of Shizuoka side from which Mt. Fuji could be seen. Indeed, it is an area that stands out the most of the Japanese archipelago, and I assume there was plenty of food. He says he landed in that area.

Hotsuma Tsutae is different from *Kojiki* and *Nihon Shoki* in that it describes that such God had existed and that Amaterasu-O-Mikami was a male god. It also says that the other two of the Three Deities—Tsukuyomi-no-Mikoto and Susanoo-no-Mikoto—were male gods, too. This theory can be possible because souls are sometimes born into a man and sometimes a woman.

2

What Kind of Being Is Ame-no-Mioya-Gami?

Why did Ame-no-Mioya-Gami not speak Japanese in his first spiritual message?

Looking at how the communication went between Ame-no-Mioya-Gami and Interviewer A in Part One, Chapter One, I feel it might make people go crazy [*laughs*]. I have no idea if this spiritual message is valuable or not. Maybe Interviewer A was teased. Given that Ame-no-Mioya-Gami spoke Japanese later (Part One, Chapter Two), perhaps he was teasing us; maybe he played us. When we recorded his spiritual message in our special lecture hall, he spoke Japanese, so maybe we were teased. He may have thought that appearing in an unexpected way for the first time would be more interesting. Later he spoke Japanese, which means he didn't speak when he could. Or maybe he was in a bad mood at that time.

There are not many people who had come from Andromeda; we have investigated very few such cases. Andromeda is over two million light-years away from here, so it is extremely far compared to the planets of others who had come from the universe. I presume not many people have come directly from the Andromeda Galaxy; many are probably born into other planetary civilizations of the Milky Way Galaxy first before coming to Earth.

The reason why Ame-no-Mioya-Gami did not speak Japanese when he first appeared was perhaps he wanted to express that he had been away from Earth for quite a while.

Ame-no-Mioya-Gami is much older than Amaterasu-O-Mikami and Ame-no-Minakanushi-no-Kami

According to *Kojiki*, Ame-no-Minakanushi-no-Kami is said to be the first god that appeared. But what if it is true that Ame-no-Mioya-Gami appeared 30,000 years ago?

In Happy Science books published in the past, we suggested that Amaterasu-O-Mikami most probably existed around 2,800 years ago, and Ame-no-Minakanushi-no-Kami was a little earlier than that—probably just before 3,000 years ago—and he appeared in the Kyushu area. We introduced such a presumption. But 30,000 years ago is much older than that. So we are not sure how many other gods had appeared between those ages.

The current Japanese emperor is the 125th emperor and the next will be the 126th (at the time of the lecture). But according to *Hotsuma Tsutae*, there are two hundred and some dozens of emperors before him, so there are a hundred more ancient emperors than what's been said now. Even so, not everything is clear because the ancient emperors are said to have lived more than 100 years or even 200 years, which is fairly long.

Takenouchi-no-Sukune, who is said to have handed down this knowledge, also lived until roughly 300 years old, according to the editorial note. This is another unclear point, but it is said that he had lived for a very long time. However, one source says that since there is no way a person could live such a long time, the name Takenouchi-no-Sukune must have been the name that was succeeded for generations, like the names for kabuki actors. Just like the names Kinnosuke Nakamura and Danjuro Ichikawa are succeeded to next generations in the world of kabuki, it says that the name Takenouchi-no-Sukune was succeeded within the Takenouchi family, and these successors handed down the story. Such a theory exists.

As a side note, the Jewish documents also mention ancient people who had lived for hundreds of years or even a thousand years. I'm not sure how much of it is true, but sometimes, people of ancient times are described in this way.

Aide to Master & CEO and a staff member had a dream of Ame-no-Mioya-Gami on the same night

How Ame-no-Mioya-Gami looked like is quite unclear, but Part One of the book has a small episode-like story of a dream that Aide to Master & CEO Shio Okawa had one night. She said she dreamed of the Ame-no-Mioya-Gami Shrine. She clearly described her dream in the following way: "On a slope were wooden corridors on both sides. Like the Hasedera Temple, corridors gradually sloped down at both sides. The middle of these corridors was an inner garden like a courtyard, and a wooden shrine probably stood at the top of the slope. A lot of people were gathering in the corridors, seemingly waiting for something. Then Ame-no-Mioya-Gami came down, walking in the middle of the path while everyone was sitting on their heels and was worshiping him. As she thought he would pass by, he stopped and started to give a sermon."

She had such a dream on July 22, 2018, and on the same morning, a staff member at Religious Affairs Headquarters also had a dream, though I'm not sure if I can say this. I've heard that she was washing very hard a gigantic wooden bathtub that was like a cypress bath for some reason in her dream. She was scrubbing the bathtub, wondering how big of a person would bathe here. By joining these two dreams, it gradually made sense. It seems that the bathtub was so huge that a giant sumo wrestler could get into. I heard that these dreams were probably connected.

Ame-no-Mioya-Gami was like a 25-meter-tall yokozuna, and was the size of the great statue of Buddha when sitting

There is sumo wrestling in Japan, and perhaps its origin could go back as far as about 30,000 years ago. Ame-no-Mioya-Gami is apparently very similar to a sumo wrestler. When described, the image of an almost naked figure wearing some cloth on his muscular body, like the statue of Kongo Rikishi, often appears. So Ame-no-Mioya-Gami may be at the origin of such statues.

I don't know how tall he exactly was. When we spoke to him on a different occasion, we asked him how tall he was, and he said he was 25-meter-tall (about 82 feet). I'm not sure if this is true; if it's true, he would be as big as a monster [*laughs*]. We thought he meant 2.5 meters instead of 25 meters, but it would be rude to ask him again, so we didn't. Given that Godzilla is 80-meter-tall (about 262 feet), perhaps he could truly be 25-meter-tall. If his offspring became smaller, it might have been because there was not enough food on Earth, and they may have grown smaller. I don't know exactly, but Ame-no-Mioya-Gami himself said he was 25-meter-tall. The image of a 25-meter-tall yokozuna is quite spectacular; when sitting, he would be just the size of the great statue of Buddha. We can assume that Ame-no-Mioya-Gami was as big as the great statue of Buddha when sitting.

Why did *Hotsuma Tsutae* become unofficial?

Takenouchi-no-Sukune seems to have written *Hotsuma Tsutae*; because it's in ancient times, maybe he received inspiration like a shaman about ancient facts from Ame-no-Mioya-Gami himself or someone else. Or it may have been passed down as oral tradition, as commonly practiced in India. I don't know exactly, but it may have remained in that way.

Hotsuma Tsutae was not considered a legitimate history book but was made unofficial; perhaps because Amaterasu-O-Mikami, who appears multiple times, is described as a male god whose empresses' names were written and also had children. Since the time before World War II, it is very likely that people already believed in Amaterasu-O-Mikami being a goddess, so I think such descriptions were not taken well.

The belief in Amaterasu-O-Mikami being a goddess was established pretty early on. Since Empress Jito was ruling the country just before the compilations of *Kojiki* and *Nihon Shoki*, one source says that faith in the goddess Amaterasu-O-Mikami was established to legitimate the female ruler. Such a theory exists, but I don't necessarily think it is true. People can be born into both male and female, so I think Amaterasu-O-Mikami's soul had been born as male or female depending on the time.

At the root of Japanese Shinto are the teachings of Ame-no-Mioya-Gami

The teachings of Ame-no-Mioya-Gami are described in Section 3 of Chapter Two in Part One.

First, he taught manners.

Second, he taught the difference between heaven and earth.

Third, he taught harmony between man and woman.

Fourth, he taught to hold ceremonies at various turning points in life. He taught to hold ceremonies at each turning point in life—such as when people get married, a baby is born, they become of age, and when they die—to have the gods recognize their milestones as their witnesses.

Fifth, he taught ritual prayers and festivals.

Sixth, he taught the heart of respect, to believe, and to learn.

Seventh, he taught order and harmony. When looking at them, you can see the basic teachings of Japanese Shinto. So we could say that his teachings are at the root of Japanese Shinto.

In the series of spiritual messages published in the early days of Happy Science, Japanese Shinto is considered to belong to the Purple Light of God, which mainly consists of the teachings of the ninth dimensional spirit Confucius of China. Japanese Shinto was said to be within the stream of Confucius' teachings. We thought that Shinto was under the influence of Confucianism because Confucianism was adopted like Japan's state religion during the Edo period, which lasted for 300 years. But this idea will be overturned. If Ame-no-Mioya-Gami is more ancient than Confucius and Japan had its own teachings that were similar to Confucianism, the truth could be the opposite; it is highly possible that Japan "exported" those teachings instead.

Looking at the ideas of Ame-no-Mioya-Gami, I think that, in general, they are not different to the teachings of Japanese Shinto. He taught bowing, order, harmony, ritual prayers, and the heart of respect—these are certainly valued by Japanese Shinto.

Hihiiro-gane is assumed to be a similar substance to the metal used for UFOs

Ame-no-Mioya-Gami also mentions the metallic substance which existed before ironware or bronzeware. It is called "hihiiro-kane," though I myself call it "hihiiro-gane." I think it was written in *Hotsuma Tsutae* and *Takenouchi Monjo* as well. They mention it many times. It is a mysterious metal, and I'm not sure what exactly it is. It is assumed to be similar to the metal used to make UFOs.

Apparently, this metal is unexpectedly light but strong; it's strong but easy to process. Once in a while, the description of such metal can be found in Japan. It is indeed a mysterious metal.

The description of this hihiro-kane often appears; it may be a kind of evidence of the universe. Such substance existed but because there wasn't much of this material, I think people gradually shifted to using stones and woods to make different kinds of things.

3

Overturning the Established Theory of the Japanese Civilization

According to Ame-no-Mioya-Gami, the Japanese civilization is older than that of Lemuria or Mu

Happy Science generally states the theory that civilizations such as the Mu civilization came into the Japanese civilization but Ame-no-Mioya-Gami says, "No, *we* are older." He says that Japan taught the civilization to Lemuria and Mu.

He also mentions Vishnu, who is thought to be the highest god of India. In the stories of Vishnu, there is one related to the genesis of the universe: When Vishnu was taking a nap and dozing off near a lotus pond or something, he saw the universe, which then became this world. There is such a big-scale story. But according to Ame-no-Mioya-Gami, Vishnu is like a mere portion of his soul, so he talks on a very large scale. His talks are so big that it makes me wonder if he might be the very origin of *tengu* (long-nosed goblins). I feel that this aspect of him significantly influenced Japanese Shinto. In this vein, he says something like Japan influenced both India and Mu, and their influence came back to Japan again after those areas sank.

"Ame-no-Minakanushi" might be the name used by those from the universe

In the past, we thought that Ame-no-Minakanushi was probably the oldest and highest god in Japanese Shinto, but a much ancient one has appeared. Indeed, Ame-no-Minakanushi-no-Kami is described in *Kojiki* as hitori-gami who doesn't seem to have reality. Shrines worshiping him are also very few in Japan. There are a few small shrines in Chiba Prefecture; they have drawings of the Big Dipper similar to one that came from the Persian area and some patterns similar to Islamic culture. There are some in Kumamoto Prefecture as well. But these shrines are very few if you look at the whole of Japan. Compared to the predominant faith in Amaterasu-O-Mikami, faith in Ame-no-Minakanushi is very limited; I think that is either because he was too old or there was no reality to his existence.

After some research, we assume that "Ame-no-Minakanushi" could be a general name for those who had come from the universe. Ame-no-Minakanushi-no-Kami literally means "god at the center of the universe," but regarding which being from the universe is unclear. So, rather than a god with human character existed as real, solid being, it is more likely that those from the universe used such a name. Ame-no-Mioya-Gami says Ame-no-Minakanushi has appeared on different occasions, but I'm not sure whether these beings are all inter-related or not. These days I perceive him that way. Even so, they are likely to have come on a flying saucer.

The reason for changing the name of the movie's main character to "Makoto Mioya"

The reason for making Part One of this book public is related to the main character's name of the movie, *Immortal Hero*, scheduled to be released this autumn (October 2019). I originally put the name Satoshi Inuyama, but the film director requested a better name, saying it was hard to feel respectful for the name Inuyama (literally meaning, "dog hill"). So I thought, "Well, he might be right." I think Inuyama is the name of a district near Nagoya City, but anyway, I named the main character "Makoto Mioya" after Ame-no-Mioya-Gami—introduced by Takenouchi-no-Sukune.

I hope the movie won't end up being unworthy of his name. We haven't conducted any spiritual message from Takenouchi-no-Sukune (at the time of the lecture), and I don't know who will appear when we summon Takenouchi-no-Sukune. If the name was succeeded for generations, we might not be able to specify who he is. But I think it's OK to use the name Makoto Mioya.

Ame-no-Mioya-Gami considers the crisis surrounding Japan now, as he talks

So, Ame-no-Mioya-Gami states the different thing from the established theory of today. He says that the Japanese archipelago became separated from the continent, and from around 30,000 years ago an advanced civilization developed and also had an influence on Mu and Lemuria, which was then reimported by Japan. He also says that the Japanese culture spread to China, Russia, and the Korean peninsula, including South Korea, as well. So it is the opposite of what is usually being said. I assume that he says this while also considering Japan's crisis today.

If it is true that Ame-no-Mioya-Gami came from Andromeda 30,000 years ago and built the basis of the current Japanese civilization, then I think there must be some grounding for what he says. But even if wooden shrines were built at the foothills of Mt. Fuji, it cannot be helped that there are no remains of them; I think they are now buried under the sea of trees at Mt. Fuji.

While Ame-no-Mioya-Gami says he came 30,000 years ago, Happy Science is talking about 300 to 400 million years ago. We haven't investigated enough about whether it was the first and last time he had come or whether there were other stories before that. Since there is a big gap, there probably are some other stories in between.

Ame-no-Mioya-Gami is possibly an 11th dimensional being, but it is still unclear

Another distinguishing feature—which is also quite a big scale—is that he says he is the being of the 11th dimension. If he is involved in larger galaxies, he could be connected to such a higher dimension, but this is also unclear. Of course, even if El Cantare is said to be the being of the Earth's ninth dimension, its central core stretches to a much higher place, and I presume it is connected to the realm of about 20th dimension. So I'm not sure which area he is talking about.

As for whether such an 11th dimensional being would truly call the interviewer, who is a senior managing director of Happy Science, "stupid," it is a little questionable. Some may find it no surprise, while others may argue, "Such a being won't use such a vulgar word. That would be more of a human-like being." I don't know for sure about this. It is impossible to disprove such an argument. There are times when you would want to say things like that. The interviewer is often told off as such, so sometimes, he may be giving out such vibrations.

In any case, we cannot take what Ame-no-Mioya-Gami says as it is. He also says he is superior to Alpha and Elohim, but I don't have enough backing to confirm it.

It is all right to assume that there was an old Japanese civilization

I think it's all right to assume that there was indeed an old Japanese civilization. If this is true, a question may arise about the kinds of civilizations that existed in between now and those times, but even if they were to be described, it would probably be very science-fiction-like stories. Nevertheless, maybe it's better to speak about such ancient times. China says they have a 5,000-year civilization. I'm not sure about the Indian civilization. How long is it? It may not be longer than 8,000 years; they say it's a little longer than 5,000 years. The Middle East is said to have a history of about 6,000 years, and Egypt has a history of 7,000 to 8,000 or even 10,000 years. So, a history of 30,000 years is very old. Well, there is such an idea.

Regarding the tale of "Urashima Taro" (see p.179), Ame-no-Mioya-Gami talks of the ring of time using the analogy of the Yamanote Line. He also talks about the parallel world, so he may be a being who can understand such matters to some extent.

In *Hotsuma Tsutae*, it is written that Ame-no-Mioya-Gami was born in Japan once. Although it does not mention the aforementioned story of him coming in a large fleet, this may be what *Hotsuma Tsutae* is referring to.

I wonder if there was an empress that married a 25-meter-tall man. I don't know exactly. There could be one if she, too, were about the same size. This is shrouded in mystery, so I don't know.

Even if I continue to talk like this, it will still be difficult to understand. So, for the remaining time, I would like to answer some questions if you have any.

CHAPTER TWO

Q&A Session

Exploring Deeper into the Secrets of Japan and the Universe

Originally recorded in Japanese on February 5, 2019
at General Headquarters, Happy Science, Japan
and later translated into English.

Q1

About the Japanese Spirit World and the Enthronement of the New Emperor

QUESTIONER 1

Thank you very much for your lecture today. I am surprised at how much of Ame-no-Mioya-Gami's trace, including his appearance, remains in Japan's civilization and culture to this day, even though he came to Japan 30,000 years ago. For example, there is a strong culture in sumo wrestler's figures and kabuki make-up. It's quite surprising. Is it because of the spiritual strength of Ame-no-Mioya-Gami?

Also, this year (2019), there will be imperial succession, and a new emperor will be enthroned. The history of the emperor had a significant influence on Japanese politics, so how should we understand the enthronement of this new emperor? I would be grateful if you could teach us on this matter.

Shakyamuni Buddha sometimes goes to teach in Andromeda

RYUHO OKAWA

There are some objections to what Ame-no-Mioya-Gami said in his spiritual messages (Part One). He spoke like he was much superior to other branch spirits of El Cantare, and he said things like *Mr.* El Miore and *Mr.* El Cantare. But when I asked Shakyamuni Buddha, he said, "Oh, Andromeda. They were very behind in terms of their culture, so I sometimes go there to educate them." Currently, Shakyamuni Buddha is mainly based on Earth, but he said, "I sometimes go to Andromeda and give guidance to raise people's awareness there. I educate *Mr.* Ame-no-Mioya-Gami." So, his (Ame-no-Mioya-Gami's) words cannot be taken straightforwardly. Indeed, looking at the level of the teachings of Japanese Shinto, Buddhism is high enough to give them teachings. So if Shakyamuni Buddha himself says that he sometimes goes out to the universe and even teaches Andromeda to raise their civilization, then that may be true. But when it comes to the debate of who is higher, I try not to take it seriously.

This shows that there are some interactions. The Indian culture was also transmitted to Japan, so we can say that various things are connected. But looking at how the teachings about the detailed, different states of mind are not taught (by Ame-no-Mioya-Gami), I think Earth is a little ahead on this point and should teach people over there (Andromeda). Andromeda has the ideas that formed the basis of Japanese Shinto, such as "getting rid of impurity and having a pure mind," "respecting the elderly," and "observing manners," and they put a premium on formality. I think the sumo wrestlers dress themselves that way to show they have nothing to hide before God. So, I believe there were teachings of a much higher level in numerous religions that arose on Earth.

Ame-no-Mioya-Gami brought customs to create a new civilization

I'm not sure whether Ame-no-Mioya-Gami is connected to the imperial family as its ancestor. I presume that people already lived in Japan 30,000 years ago, and space people descended there and brought things that helped create a new civilization. They probably taught people things like shrines and how to carry out religious ceremonies. People built wooden shrines like Ame-no-Mioya-Gami Shrine, and he descended from there.

God walks in the middle of the path—this is still said now in shrines, including Ise Jingu Shrine and Meiji Jingu Shrine. If this custom also existed back then, what Ame-no-Mioya-Gami says makes sense. What he says accords with the custom today, so I think it was him who brought in such a custom.

The views of the Japanese Spirit World contain many elements from the "rear side" of the Spirit World

I still need to explore more about the Japanese Spirit World. We Happy Science get a lot of information related to bodhisattvas and angels. Still, as you can see from the Japanese manga *GeGeGe no Kitaro* and Hayao Miyazaki's animation, many *yokai* (monsters and goblins) appear in the Japanese Spirit World. It's full of yokai. But not many yokai appear before me because I don't have many "friends" who are yokai. I think they live in a different world.

Normally, their world is rather small but I think it is quite vast and has a bigger share in the Japanese Spirit World. Most of the books by the founder of Oomoto-kyo religion Onisaburo Deguchi are about the worlds of yokai, *sennin* (hermits), and tengu; they describe many stories about how foxes shape-shift and deceive each other. There are many descriptions about the world similar to the so-called traditional Japanese Spirit World. So I think that part of the world has a big domain.

Although the Japanese Spirit World modernized slightly with the introduction of Buddhism, a fight goes on regarding this matter even after Meiji Restoration (in the 19th century). The world of yokai is declining, but the mainstream "front side" of the Spirit World has not yet expanded enough. Even so, the Japanese Spirit World is slightly westernized and can now partly interact with the Western Spirit World.

In the ideas of Japanese Shinto, there is faith that can be described simply and orderly as stated by Ame-no-Mioya-Gami, and I think they perform "front side" rituals following that faith. But regarding the content of faith, many elements that seem to come from the "rear side" (of the Spirit World) are included in Shinto views of the Spirit World. I think this is where Japanese Shinto is somehow preventing Japan from modernizing itself.

There are also Western-style monotheistic religions. The teachings of monotheistic religions clearly distinguish good and evil, and some of them teach about the challenges of humans' soul training, and the direction humans should head into. In this sense, I feel they are certainly more advanced.

Japanese animism is in the stream that came from India

In addition to this world of yokai, there is an idea that says, "All nature is god." This is called "animism"—the belief that mountains, rivers, plants, and trees are all gods of Japan. Everything is regarded as god.

Mr. Takeshi Umehara, a Japanese philosopher who recently passed away, said something along the lines of, "Animism is, in fact, Japan's true faith, and the State Shinto in Meiji era and onward is wrong in that it tried to establish monotheism forcibly. They tried to make Japan a monotheistic country by making the emperor a living god. It's unforgivable that they tried to dismiss Buddhism by destroying its temples, statues, and sutras and oppressed other Shinto denominations. What is worse, their concept of 'god' is wrong. Japan is not a monotheistic country. It used to have animism in which people believed that gods exist in all kinds of places, whether it be pebbles, trees, mountains, or rivers. But the Meiji Restoration 'killed' such a faith." He stubbornly insisted on such an idea.

But animism is actually in the stream of Indian thoughts, from which Buddhism was handed down. India also has such an idea, and there are many gods. They don't say there are eight million gods like we do in Japan, but India is generally said to be a polytheistic country. They have Vishnu at the center. Vishnu has about 10 faces, just like Kannon or Avalokitesvara (goddess of mercy), and it is said that one of his faces is Shakyamuni Buddha. People in India seem to understand that Shakyamuni Buddha is like a part of Vishnu's soul.

Other than Vishnu, there are Shiva—god of war, or god of destruction—and minor gods such as monkey god, elephant god Ganesha, and bird god or god of mysterious bird Garuda. It is true that in those areas, large eagles fly; they dive down, catch the snake on the earth and eat it. Garuda-like birds are considered guardian deities in Buddhism. Sometimes, snakes are also regarded as guardian deities. Because of the legendary stories, snakes are enshrined in Venuvana monastery and Bodh Gaya. It is said that a large cobra spread its head wide to become like an umbrella to shelter Shakyamuni Buddha from the rain while meditating.

In reality, cobras are very dangerous for the practitioners of Buddhist training, and many practitioners lost their lives by being bitten by a cobra as they underwent spiritual training in the forest. So it is questionable whether snakes can be called guardian deities. But like in Japanese Shinto, people in India perhaps tended to enshrine scary creatures. So, snakes are also considered the guardian deities of Buddhism and are called "Naga." They were then changed to be considered dragons and were sublimated to be dragon gods.

In this way, there are many gods in India, and so are in Japan. If we explore the Spirit World, there are indeed all kinds of beings. So it is not surprising that those with divine powers or supernatural powers, which people on earth don't have, are regarded as gods.

The tales of "Princess Kaguya" and "Urashima Taro" are most likely universe-related stories

This was written in Part One of this book, but Sukunahikona-no-Mikoto of Izumo region was ignored in *Kojiki* and *Nihon Shoki*. However, his name often appears in the local history books called *Fudoki*, which existed before *Kojiki* and *Nihon Shoki*. In today's terms he is exactly like the Avengers' Ant-Man; he is a small god the size of a thumb but does many great things. There are descriptions about such a god that is like the origin of Ant-Man. Perhaps his existence has been handed down in the form of a folktale, like "Issun Boshi" ("The One-Inch Boy").

There is also a tale called "Princess Kaguya." An old man finds a shining bamboo in a bamboo forest. Wondering what it is, he cuts down the bamboo and finds a little girl of about four inches. He then finds many gold coins as well. Perhaps a brave little alien came to Earth carrying "childcare expenses." So he finds Princess Kaguya as small as about four inches with an extra gift of gold coin, or "dowry." He brings her home, and in less than a year—just a few months—she becomes an adult. This is like a panda because a panda grows up within one or two years. Princess Kaguya grows up at such a speed.

The story also talks of how various important men of the city propose to Princess Kaguya after she reaches adulthood. While she makes them compete with each other and refuses the proposals, she starts to say things like, "I must return home now," or "Emissaries will come for me from the moon." Sure enough, with Shakyamuni Buddha or Amitabha Buddha-like person at the center and a bodhisattva-like person behind him, many emissaries come down on clouds from the sky to take her while playing music with flute and drums. Having known this, hundreds of soldiers are there to protect Princess Kaguya, but when the emissaries from the moon arrive, everyone becomes unable to move or fire an arrow.

Not being able to move is indeed very similar to an alien phenomenon. It is often reported that you can't move your body or experience sleep paralysis at the time of the alien abduction. So surprisingly, I think the story accurately tells the incident. A report tells such an incident that occurred around the time *Kojiki* and *Nihon Shoki* were completed, or during the Heian period (794-1185). So it is possible that such an incident—the "Princess Kaguya incident"—did occur. I presume that a tiny being came from the universe, suddenly grew big by getting used to the Earth's life, then returned to the moon. I think things like this happened in reality because the depiction incredibly resembles the alien phenomenon.

The same is true with the stories of "Umisachi Yamasachi" and "Urashima Taro." In the latter legend, the protagonist Taro goes to Ryugu-jo palace under the sea, enjoys and lives there happily for three years, but when he returns home, 300 years have gone by. As he opens the treasure box, smoke comes out, and he turns into an old man. He also visits his parents' old house and finds that it was a thing of hundreds of years ago. So his three years in Ryugu-jo becomes 300 years on the earth. This story seems as if Taro went on a space travel. Maybe he journeyed to outer space and went to some water planet. Since ancient times, there have been many such universe-related stories.

My spiritual dream about boarding on a UFO with the former U.S. President Bush

This goes off topic, but since I mentioned the spiritual dream about Ame-no-Mioya-Gami earlier, I will talk about mine as well. There is no specific academic material on him, so I think it's better I go off topic a little. Speaking of the spiritual dream, I also had one. I think it was around November last year (2018). I seldom get abducted, so this was quite rare, but I experienced something that could be called an abduction. It was between 2:00 am and 3:00 am. I found myself on a big spaceship. I was on something like a mother ship bigger than the usual UFO, and it was about to land. We landed on some planet, a very green place with widespread pastureland. When disembarking, one side of the flying saucer opened wide, which became like a passage or steps to descend. So I got off onto the pastureland and found I was with someone else. It was the former U.S. President Bush. Bush senior—the father—was with his wife, Barbara.

Bush senior came to Japan after the Gulf War. I think it was around 1992. When he came to Japan, he played tennis with the Crown Prince Naruhito—the next emperor (at the time of the lecture)—and others during the daytime. The crown prince was very good at tennis, and apparently, the president lost big. That night, Mr. Bush attended the dinner party, and it was aired on TV. But during dinner, he went unconscious and collapsed. The first lady, Barbara tried to save the situation by saying something like, "He fell because he lost the tennis match. His partner ambassador was too weak." I remember watching such a scene on TV. So President Bush fainted during the dinner because, as it was told, he lost at tennis and was tired.

The president going unconscious is not a very good thing; I think that scene was aired on CNN or some other channels. The approval rating of President Bush reached as high as 90 percent by the time the U.S. side coalition forces won the Gulf War, and he was naturally expected to be re-elected as the president. But after he collapsed in Japan and his collapse was aired, he was suddenly regarded as being embarrassing, giving way to young Clinton to become the next president. Such a thing happened. He should have won the election with an approval rating of 90 percent but lost because of such an embarrassing incident.

Anyway, I had the dream. It left me with the feeling, "It's strange. I seldom have a dream traveling with the U.S. president and the first lady, so it's strange." Then, within that month, President Bush passed away. I didn't know about his condition, but around that time, he was probably in the hospital, almost in a vegetative state. He was already in a very bad condition, and I think Mrs. Bush had already passed away.

Going back to the story of my dream, three of us were on board. Although I wasn't quite sure which planet it was, the UFO opened there, and we were dropped off. We saw a field where there were 16 cows. Like how it is often depicted in the abduction scenes, 16 cows were there. Two cows were passed out foaming from the mouth, one of which was a Japanese Awa cow. I don't know why but I knew it was the Awa cow from Tokushima Prefecture. It was lying on the field foaming, but I wasn't sure about the other one. I just knew clearly that one Awa cow was fallen over on the field. I couldn't figure out the breed of the other cows. They were in good shape and were eating grass. I clearly remember that I landed there with Mr. and Mrs. Bush. I also remember talking about it to Ms. Shio (Aide to Master & CEO) in the middle of the night.

Former President Bush passed away within that one month, so I thought to myself, "Oh, maybe we truly went there together. He may have had an out-of-body experience and was also invited to go there." Perhaps he was taken because he was thought to have never boarded on one (UFO). But it's shameful that only the Awa cow was fallen over foaming. I thought there was some intention behind it, but I couldn't figure it out.

Incidentally, back when I was still a student, I got a job offer from a trading house, so I would visit the company until I officially entered it. At that time, a person from the human resources division gave me a nickname, "Raging bull of Awa." There was a time where I was called by the nickname "Raging bull of Awa," but it may have been sarcasm.

So I had such a dream. It was very real; the green was vivid, and the cows' white and black pattern was clear. I clearly saw a cow foaming from the mouth and heard people calling former President Bush and his wife, Barbara. Probably it was in the form of an out-of-body experience. I think I didn't go there with my physical body but was taken as an out-of-body experience. I had such an experience around November last year (2018).

Both the Japanese administration and the imperial family may experience tough situations from now on

Regarding your question about what will happen after the change in the imperial family, I think people now have higher expectations for the new change. Prime Minister Abe is probably expecting to further accelerate the "Abe bubble" with the economic recovery and next year's (2020)

Olympics (at the time of the lecture). I shouldn't say too much because I shouldn't disappoint them, but according to what I've heard from various space people, this year and even after will be tough. They all say that things are going to be tough. However, they also say, "The fact that tough situations continue doesn't necessarily mean there are headwinds for you." Although tough, tough means we have a job, a mission. Nevertheless, they say that both the Japanese administration and the imperial family may experience pretty tough situations. So we could face a so-called "national crisis."

There could be domestic and international concerns, and in terms of domestic concerns, the imperial family is currently swaying a lot. There will be the Emperor Emeritus, and various troubles are likely to arise regarding his grandchildren. So, people's respect, or the feeling similar to faith toward the imperial family, will waver. To be more precise, people may start to feel that the imperial family members are just like them and like ordinary human beings. If there is such a wavering, arguments could arise over money—whether it is good or bad to use tax to conduct the many rituals they perform. Even Prince Akishino said certain rituals should be done with private funds, not public funds. This remark caused a little stir and is called a "rebellion of Prince Akishino." So, the imperial family may be shaken a little.

Prince Akishino will be the crown prince, and he will be the first in line for succession. So should anything happen to the next emperor, Prince Akishino could be the emperor. The current emperor being retired means a new system is being made that allows an emperor to abdicate during his life. Only the Akishinonomiya family has a boy, and Crown Prince Naruhito only has a girl. According to Imperial House Law, the imperial throne must be succeeded by imperial male descendants. So if Prince Akishino wants his son to succeed, he should be the emperor by having the current Crown Prince Naruhito abdicate and become the emperor emeritus during his life. Or should indisposition or something happens to the crown prince, and he is no longer able to work as the head of the imperial family, Prince Akishino could accede to the emperor. He may be thinking about maintaining the male-line succession in this way in case such an event happens.

If we think like this, we can more or less understand why Prince Akishino said something along the lines of, "Spending ¥2.2 billion (about US$19 million) of public funds was too much to perform Daijosai ritual at the start of the Heisei era. It should be done more simply using private funds." Maybe he is implying, "Your reign will be short, so do it cheap. The rest will come around to me," and might be testing his elder brother's reaction. If this is the case, his remark makes sense logically. He might be saying, "We will properly maintain Japanese imperial lineage, so just don't spend too much money." I feel such an intention, so some troubles might arise between the brothers or between the parents and the child.

About the relationship between the emperor of the Heisei era and the Abe administration

This is just a guess, but I presume the current emperor (now emperor emeritus) is at odds with the Abe administration after Mr. Abe came back in office as prime minister in the Heisei era. The emperor is not supposed to tell his true thoughts, but I think his feelings were closer to the past three prime ministers of the Democratic Party administration. When he was young, he was taught the anti-war, pacifist views such as "observing the Constitution," "maintaining the article 9 of the Constitution," and "adhering to pacifism." When Japan was occupied, he even felt danger for life. So presumably, his thoughts are closer to the Constitutional Democratic Party.

Therefore, his abdication during his lifetime may be partly due to his unwillingness to see Mr. Abe's face, though there may be some other reasons as well. I think part of the reason is that he doesn't want to go to the Diet and deliver his words every time the Diet is convened. I say this because the emperor once delayed the opening of the Diet session for three days. He was in Hayama Imperial Villa for rest and recuperation, and asking him to return for the opening of the Diet session was considered rude. So I remember the call for the Diet session was postponed for three days. I have never seen such a case. So perhaps the emperor didn't want to see Mr. Abe's face because he didn't like what Mr. Abe was working on. It seems like the current emperor sees that Japan is slowly moving toward militarizing itself, and in this sense, he probably doesn't want to continue being an emperor anymore. This may sound rude, but maybe it is one form of "boycotting."

Assuming the Crown Princess Masako (the current empress) will be the "advisor" to the next emperor, we are unsure about how the next emperor and empress will handle things.

The freedom of religion should be maintained

It is said that one of the past lives of Crown Prince Naruhito is the person defeated at the battle of Dan-no-ura (1185), and his mother at the time—Kenreimon-in, who threw herself in the sea upon the fall of Heike (the Taira clan)—is Empress Michiko (the current empress emerita). This was confirmed in our past spiritual research. So there is a possibility that some kind of crisis may hit the imperial family. But I feel they have no choice but to moderately handle difficult management situations while struggling with democracy.

Ame-no-Mioya-Gami and Amaterasu-O-Mikami appear at Happy Science, so if this is openly and solidly approved, our relation to the imperial family will be very difficult. If we cannot exist within the scope of religious freedom, there will be problems. If there were a monotheistic faith in the emperor like the pre-World War II period, Happy Science would definitely be oppressed. So I think it's better for them to remain lightly as a symbol, without going too far. I will say no more because there could be some trouble.

I have no idea about the next era name because it is now under discussion (at the time of the lecture). But some hint could be found in the policy speech of Prime Minister Abe given at the beginning of this year, in which he seemed to suggestively quote from ancient Chinese literature. He used the word "tensei," meaning "achieving heaven." Now is the Heisei era, meaning "achieving peace." "Achieving heaven" can mean achieving or realizing heaven's will, so I'm guessing Mr. Abe likes such a kind of word. It seems the ideas are now narrowed down to three options, and the new era name will be announced on April 1.[1]

While it's better for us not to criticize the imperial family too much, I don't want them to bring back the monotheistic-like State Shinto as they did in the past. Because of the idea, "the separation of religion and state," Happy Science is now against the headwind. But if Japan's national structure is based on the imperial family or if the emperor is regarded as the living god like the pre-war period, they will probably clash with El Cantare-belief. Although State Shinto called itself not a religion, there were times when they oppressed other religions. Therefore, to prevent such oppression from happening again, the separation of religion and state was set by the Constitution after World War II. This is how I understand it. I hope freedom of religion will be maintained. I can only say things vaguely on the matter, but this is how I feel at the moment.

Q2

How Far Can the Secrets of the God of the Universe Be Revealed?

QUESTIONER 2

Thank you very much for the precious opportunity today. You mentioned in the lecture the relationship between Lord El Cantare and Ame-no-Mioya-Gami. Also, we were already given the spiritual messages from Lord Heem of Vega. We learn these things but we cannot really understand their relationship to each other and their roles. Maybe it is El Cantare who unifies them all as the God of the universe. I would be very grateful if you could teach us about the secrets around such matters as far as we are allowed to know.

Our relation to the universe is getting very close now

RYUHO OKAWA

This is quite a difficult area. Until now, I've taught for about 30 years that Earth has the Spirit World consisting of the fourth dimension, the fifth dimension, the sixth dimension, the seventh dimension, the eighth dimension, and the ninth dimension, and it surrounds Earth in an onion-shape. However, around summer last year (2018) or a little earlier, our relation to the universe has been getting close considerably. I think this happened as scheduled. Now that Happy Science has become established quite firmly as a religion, it is probably trying to step into the next stage.

It is as if a "hole" is opening up and a pillar is about to stand in the Earth's Spirit World when it was almost set with the ninth dimension. I think we are beginning to contact with yet higher dimensions and the Spirit World of the universe.

We will construct our teachings about space people based on the trust in our worldly teachings

If this goes too far and we rush too much, we could be regarded as a weird religion. So basically, we need to make sure we have sound worldly teachings and the correct historical views. Based on this trust, I think we can construct our teachings on the "Laws of the Universe"—talks about space people and how our Spirit World is connected to the higher realms of the Spirit World of the universe.

After Ame-no-Mioya-Gami said in the spiritual messages (in Part One) that he was from the 11th dimension, Lord Heem of Vega said things like he was from about the 13th dimension. If they start to compete with each other, they may possibly start saying a lot of things like this [*laughs*]. So, we just need to understand things as "That's how they said." I think it's safer not to investigate too much for now.

Ame-no-Mioya-Gami seems to be involved in other civilizations of the universe, so he may appear again when necessary. It seems he is watching the situation.

Things are becoming interconnected. Until now, we have received the revelation mainly from the spirits of higher dimensions, but now, space people have appeared and started to send us messages, although this entails some risk.

About the spiritual messages from the alien called Bashar

In the U.S., Darryl Anka is famous for bringing out an alien. What was that alien called? Does anyone remember?

A MAN FROM THE AUDIENCE
It's Bashar.

RYUHO OKAWA

Yes, it's Bashar. There was a TV program featuring the spiritual messages from aliens. I saw the image of something like the spiritual messages from Bashar, in which Darryl suddenly starts saying, "O, o, o," while sitting. He has also published books, but they are not very different from each other, and the contents are not very extensive to be called "teachings." He seems to be receiving spiritual messages from an alien, but how should I put it? His messages may be at the same level as the spiritual messages from Silver Birch that came out decades ago, or a little more simplified version. There is such a person in our contemporary.

In terms of the content, Happy Science has far richer material, so it is completely different. Also, while he (Darryl Anka) can only communicate with one alien, Happy Science can communicate with multiple beings. Even so, his contact with an alien is probably true.

A song inspired by Paul McCartney's space soul

Among those who had come to Earth, I think some have "dipped one leg into the universe" or have part of their souls live in other areas of the universe. These people can be found among those who have a very big influence on Earth or those who used to be very influential religious leaders. Some of these people probably have something like "space souls."

Recently, we have found that The Beatles' Paul McCartney seems to have a space soul, not just the soul siblings confined to Earth. He is now 76 years old (at the time of the lecture) and still alive, and sometimes holds a concert at Tokyo Dome. That Paul McCartney's space soul urged us to investigate more into John Lennon, which is how the spiritual message (from John Lennon) came out (refer to *John Lennon's Message from Heaven*).

Just yesterday (February 4, 2019), too, I recorded a song titled "Inspiration" for one of Happy Science's movies by stating it's inspired by Paul McCartney's guardian spirit. Because it was written as "Paul McCartney's guardian spirit," one of my secretaries came to ask me, "Does this mean the

John Lennon's Message from Heaven
(Tokyo: HS Press, 2020)

branch spirit of The Beatles' Paul McCartney on the earth? Or is it the one from the universe?" So I said, "Oh, it's actually a space being." I put it "guardian spirit" because mentioning a space being for songs would make things complicated, but the song was actually sent from the spaceship. This song will be used in the movie, *The Cherry Bushido*, which will be released in a few years (executive producer and original story by Ryuho Okawa, to be released in 2022). We can now receive inspiration for songs even from non-earthlings—space beings. Lord Heem was also singing. Such beings have started to make contact.

So, those who had a large, global-level influence in different ways are probably connected to the universe as well.

John Lennon met an alien while alive

Also recently, we've heard that John Lennon, too, met an alien while he was still alive. This was mentioned in supplementary information for the Happy Science movie, *The Laws of the Universe - Part 0* (Executive Producer Ryuho Okawa, released in 2015). He saw a UFO that appeared in the sky and met an alien in the Dakota Apartments, where he lived and was later shot. John Lennon said it was an insect-like alien.

When we asked him (in his spiritual message), he said that it was like an insect, something like a beetle or a rhinoceros beetle [*laughs*]. He also said the alien gave him a golden ball-like thing, which he gave to the famous psychic Uri Geller when he met him and chatted.

Even an alien went to see John Lennon before he was killed, so he was somehow connected to the universe. Like his work, when something spreads among hundreds of millions of people on Earth, I presume that some kind of influential power is coming down from the universe. Without such powers, I don't think it would spread. Happy Science is still weak in spreading our movement, so I believe we need to have more "electric current" flow in from the universe for us to spread more.

Messages from the universe will provide us with hints for the future

I don't know how far we can explore. But we must properly manage our organization and create a solid foundation. We must make sound judgments about worldly matters and show that we have not gone mad. Then, for those who want to enjoy, we will show the additional secrets like the icing on the cake, saying, "If we extend our teachings, we can teach about such world as well." I think it's better to take this approach.

I believe that messages from the universe will provide us with many hints for the future or how the future should be.

As for how much I am involved as the God of the universe or as the space soul, I myself have not yet fully grasped. As I am now living on earth with a physical body, I can't—how can I put it—travel around this universe completely freely. But I think things will come out little by little. I hope I can uncover everything, but sometimes I worry that I might have dementia by the time I have uncovered everything [*laughs*], so I want to carefully pick the right timing to reveal things.

The messages from Ame-no-Mioya-Gami can be used to convert South and North Korea and China

At least the messages from Ame-no-Mioya-Gami (Part One) alone can be used to convert South Korea, North Korea, and China in an indirect way. If they say they have a 5,000-year history, we can refute them, saying, "We have a 30,000-year history." We can also add, "We were the ones who taught you rice cultivation." South Korea—North Korea also—

claim that everything of the Japanese civilization came from around China, through the Korean peninsula. They keep on claiming, "That's why we are superior," and try to unify as a country by taking the anti-Japanese stance. So these messages can be used to crush their logic.

Even Europe and the U.S. probably wonder why such a small country like Japan has momentum and strength compared to many other Eastern countries. (The guardian spirit of) Ms. Merkel of Germany now visits me to express her wish for Japan to take care of the EU and Germany (at the time of the lecture). She may wonder why she should come over to the East and beg for help to such a small country, but I think there is something different in Japan. This difference did not only emerge after Meiji Restoration, but actually, it is probably because of Japan's pride in having a much ancient civilization.

The Japanese religious leader Mr. Onisaburo Deguchi wrote *Reikai Monogatari* ("Tales of the Spirit World"), which has about 80 volumes in total. It was given orally and was transcribed. Mr. Masaharu Taniguchi also joined the group of transcription when he was working for him as a writer. I think Mr. Wasaburo Asano was involved, too. The book is not very interesting, so I myself have not read it all, but it includes the story about how the king of Judea and other kings came to greet the ancient emperor of Japan. This shows that during the ancient dynasty era, Japan was already interacting with foreign countries. I'm not sure how credible this story is, but it may be possible if UFOs were flying in those times. Or maybe it is a story that happened in the Spirit World. I don't know exactly, but the book describes such a story.

There are many mysteries, but if there is anything that can be uncovered, I would like to lay it out as much as possible. This concludes my lecture.

EDITOR'S NOTE

1 On April 1, 2019, the new era name was announced as Reiwa, meaning "beautiful harmony."

Afterword

The literal meaning of the name, Ame-no-Mioya-Gami, is "Heavenly Father" and "the Creator." His story will not be complete by this book alone. My other books describe how Ame-no-Mioya-Gami is at the origin of *bushido* (samurai spirit) of Japan (and, sometimes, of other countries). In any case, his existence explains why Japan was chosen as the birthplace of El Cantare.

Justice, propriety, order, and harmony—such words come out of Ame-no-Mioya-Gami, one after another. Over 30 years ago, I used to think that China's Confucianism influenced the teachings of Japanese Shinto. However, it is more correct to understand that Confucianism was influenced by the teachings of Ame-no-Mioya-Gami but failed to incorporate his spiritual thoughts.

Whatever the case, I believe that blowing away the dark clouds of today's China is also the mission of Happy Science.

Ryuho Okawa
Master & CEO of Happy Science Group
February 2, 2021

For a deeper understanding of
Part One "The Descent of Japanese Father God Ame-no-Mioya-Gami"
see other books below by Ryuho Okawa:

The Laws of the Sun [New York: IRH Press, 2018]

The Laws of Faith [New York: IRH Press, 2018]

My Journey through the Spirit World [New York: IRH Press, 2018]

The Truth About World War II [Tokyo: HS Press, 2015]

The following book is only available at Happy Science locations. Please see the contact information on pp. 264-265.

The Laws of Alpha [Tokyo: Happy Science, 2014]

For a deeper understanding of
Part Two "Lecture on *The Descent of Ame-no-Mioya-Gami*"
see other books below by Ryuho Okawa:

The Laws of the Sun [New York: IRH Press, 2018]

The Golden Laws [Tokyo: HS Press, 2015]

The Laws of Steel [New York: IRH Press, 2020]

John Lennon's Message from Heaven [Tokyo: HS Press, 2020]

ABOUT THE AUTHOR

Founder and CEO of Happy Science Group.

Ryuho Okawa was born on July 7th 1956, in Tokushima, Japan. After graduating from the University of Tokyo with a law degree, he joined a Tokyo-based trading house. While working at its New York headquarters, he studied international finance at the Graduate Center of the City University of New York. In 1981, he attained Great Enlightenment and became aware that he is El Cantare with a mission to bring salvation to all humankind.

In 1986, he established Happy Science. It now has members in over 165 countries across the world, with more than 700 branches and temples as well as 10,000 missionary houses around the world.

He has given over 3,400 lectures (of which more than 150 are in English) and published over 3,000 books (of which more than 600 are Spiritual Interview Series), and many are translated into 40 languages. Along with *The Laws of the Sun* and *The Laws Of Messiah*, many of the books have become best sellers or million sellers. To date, Happy Science has produced 25 movies. The original story and original concept were given by the Executive Producer Ryuho Okawa. He has also composed music and written lyrics of over 450 pieces.

Moreover, he is the Founder of Happy Science University and Happy Science Academy (Junior and Senior High School), Founder and President of the Happiness Realization Party, Founder and Honorary Headmaster of Happy Science Institute of Government and Management, Founder of IRH Press Co., Ltd., and the Chairperson of NEW STAR PRODUCTION Co., Ltd. and ARI Production Co., Ltd.

WHAT IS EL CANTARE?

El Cantare means "the Light of the Earth," and is the Supreme God of the Earth who has been guiding humankind since the beginning of Genesis. He is whom Jesus called Father and Muhammad called Allah, and is *Ame-no-Mioya-Gami*, Japanese Father God. Different parts of El Cantare's core consciousness have descended to Earth in the past, once as Alpha and another as Elohim. His branch spirits, such as Shakyamuni Buddha and Hermes, have descended to Earth many times and helped to flourish many civilizations. To unite various religions and to integrate various fields of study in order to build a new civilization on Earth, a part of the core consciousness has descended to Earth as Master Ryuho Okawa.

Alpha is a part of the core consciousness of El Cantare who descended to Earth around 330 million years ago. Alpha preached Earth's Truths to harmonize and unify Earth-born humans and space people who came from other planets.

Elohim is a part of El Cantare's core consciousness who descended to Earth around 150 million years ago. He gave wisdom, mainly on the differences of light and darkness, good and evil.

Ame-no-Mioya-Gami (Japanese Father God) is the Creator God and the Father God who appears in the ancient literature, *Hotsuma Tsutae*. It is believed that He descended on the foothills of Mt. Fuji about 30,000 years ago and built the Fuji dynasty, which is the root of the Japanese civilization. With justice as the central pillar, Ame-no-Mioya-Gami's teachings spread to ancient civilizations of other countries in the world.

Shakyamuni Buddha was born as a prince into the Shakya Clan in India around 2,600 years ago. When he was 29 years old, he renounced the world and sought enlightenment. He later attained Great Enlightenment and founded Buddhism.

Hermes is one of the 12 Olympian gods in Greek mythology, but the spiritual Truth is that he taught the teachings of love and progress around 4,300 years ago that became the origin of the current Western civilization. He is a hero that truly existed.

Ophealis was born in Greece around 6,500 years ago and was the leader who took an expedition to as far as Egypt. He is the God of miracles, prosperity, and arts, and is known as Osiris in the Egyptian mythology.

Rient Arl Croud was born as a king of the ancient Incan Empire around 7,000 years ago and taught about the mysteries of the mind. In the heavenly world, he is responsible for the interactions that take place between various planets.

Thoth was an almighty leader who built the golden age of the Atlantic civilization around 12,000 years ago. In the Egyptian mythology, he is known as god Thoth.

Ra Mu was a leader who built the golden age of the civilization of Mu around 17,000 years ago. As a religious leader and a politician, he ruled by uniting religion and politics.

WHAT IS A SPIRITUAL MESSAGE?

We are all spiritual beings living on this earth. The following is the mechanism behind Master Ryuho Okawa's spiritual messages.

1 You are a spirit

People are born into this world to gain wisdom through various experiences and return to the other world when their lives end. We are all spirits and repeat this cycle in order to refine our souls.

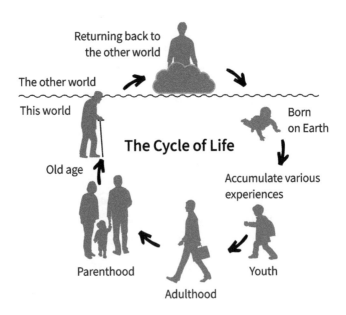

Returning back to the other world

The other world

This world

Born on Earth

The Cycle of Life

Old age

Accumulate various experiences

Parenthood

Adulthood

Youth

2 You have a guardian spirit

Guardian spirits are those who protect the people who are living on this earth. Each of us has a guardian spirit that watches over us and guides us from the other world. They were us in our past life, and are identical in how we think.

3 How spiritual messages work

Master Ryuho Okawa, through his enlightenment, is capable of summoning any spirit from anywhere in the world, including the spirit world.

Master Okawa's way of receiving spiritual messages is fundamentally different from that of other psychic mediums who undergo trances and are thereby completely taken over by the spirits they are channeling.

Master Okawa's attainment of a high level of enlightenment enables him to retain full control of his consciousness and body throughout the duration of the spiritual message. To allow the spirits to express their own thoughts and personalities freely, however, Master Okawa usually softens the dominancy of his consciousness. This way, he is able to keep his own philosophies out of the way and ensure that the spiritual messages are pure expressions of the spirits he is channeling.

Since guardian spirits think at the same subconscious level as the person living on earth, Master Okawa can summon the spirit and find out what the person on earth is actually thinking. If the person has already returned to the other world, the spirit can give messages to the people living on earth through Master Okawa.

Since 2009, many spiritual messages have been openly recorded by Master Okawa and published. Spiritual messages from the guardian spirits of people living today such as Donald Trump, former Japanese Prime Minister Shinzo Abe and Chinese President Xi Jinping, as well as spiritual messages sent from the spirit world by Jesus Christ, Muhammad, Thomas Edison, Mother Teresa, Steve Jobs and Nelson Mandela are just a tiny pack of spiritual messages that were published so far.

Domestically, in Japan, these spiritual messages are being read by a wide range of politicians and mass media, and the high-level contents of these books are delivering an impact even more on politics, news and public opinion. In recent years, there have been spiritual messages recorded in English, and

English translations are being done on the spiritual messages given in Japanese. These have been published overseas, one after another, and have started to shake the world.

① The guardian spirit / spirit in the other world...

② Goes inside Master Okawa in this world

③ Master Okawa speaks the words of the guardian spirit / spirit

For more about spiritual messages and a complete list of books in the Spiritual Interview Series, visit okawabooks.com

ABOUT HAPPY SCIENCE

Happy Science is a global movement that empowers individuals to find purpose and spiritual happiness and to share that happiness with their families, societies, and the world. With more than 12 million members around the world, Happy Science aims to increase awareness of spiritual truths and expand our capacity for love, compassion, and joy so that together we can create the kind of world we all wish to live in.

Activities at Happy Science are based on the Principle of Happiness (Love, Wisdom, Self-Reflection, and Progress). This principle embraces worldwide philosophies and beliefs, transcending boundaries of culture and religions.

Love teaches us to give ourselves freely without expecting anything in return; it encompasses giving, nurturing, and forgiving.

Wisdom leads us to the insights of spiritual truths, and opens us to the true meaning of life and the will of God (the universe, the highest power, Buddha).

Self-Reflection brings a mindful, nonjudgmental lens to our thoughts and actions to help us find our truest selves—the essence of our souls—and deepen our connection to the highest power. It helps us attain a clean and peaceful mind and leads us to the right life path.

Progress emphasizes the positive, dynamic aspects of our spiritual growth—actions we can take to manifest and spread happiness around the world. It's a path that not only expands our soul growth, but also furthers the collective potential of the world we live in.

PROGRAMS AND EVENTS

The doors of Happy Science are open to all. We offer a variety of programs and events, including self-exploration and self-growth programs, spiritual seminars, meditation and contemplation sessions, study groups, and book events.

Our programs are designed to:
* Deepen your understanding of your purpose and meaning in life
* Improve your relationships and increase your capacity to love unconditionally
* Attain peace of mind, decrease anxiety and stress, and feel positive
* Gain deeper insights and a broader perspective on the world
* Learn how to overcome life's challenges
  ... and much more.

For more information, visit <u>happy-science.org</u>.

CONTACT INFORMATION

Happy Science is a worldwide organization with branches and temples around the globe. For a comprehensive list, visit the worldwide directory at *happy-science.org*. The following are some of the many Happy Science locations:

UNITED STATES AND CANADA

New York
79 Franklin St., New York, NY 10013, USA
Phone: 1-212-343-7972
Fax: 1-212-343-7973
Email: ny@happy-science.org
Website: happyscience-usa.org

New Jersey
66 Hudson St., #2R, Hoboken, NJ 07030, USA
Phone: 1-201-313-0127
Email: nj@happy-science.org
Website: happyscience-usa.org

Chicago
2300 Barrington Rd., Suite #400,
Hoffman Estates, IL 60169, USA
Phone: 1-630-937-3077
Email: chicago@happy-science.org
Website: happyscience-usa.org

Florida
5208 8th St., Zephyrhills, FL 33542, USA
Phone: 1-813-715-0000
Fax: 1-813-715-0010
Email: florida@happy-science.org
Website: happyscience-usa.org

Atlanta
1874 Piedmont Ave., NE Suite 360-C
Atlanta, GA 30324, USA
Phone: 1-404-892-7770
Email: atlanta@happy-science.org
Website: happyscience-usa.org

San Francisco
525 Clinton St. Redwood City, CA 94062, USA
Phone & Fax: 1-650-363-2777
Email: sf@happy-science.org
Website: happyscience-usa.org

Los Angeles
1590 E. Del Mar Blvd., Pasadena, CA 91106, USA
Phone: 1-626-395-7775
Fax: 1-626-395-7776
Email: la@happy-science.org
Website: happyscience-usa.org

Orange County
16541 Gothard St. Suite 104
Huntington Beach, CA 92647
Phone: 1-714-659-1501
Email: oc@happy-science.org
Website: happyscience-usa.org

San Diego
7841 Balboa Ave. Suite #202
San Diego, CA 92111, USA
Phone: 1-626-395-7775
Fax: 1-626-395-7776
E-mail: sandiego@happy-science.org
Website: happyscience-usa.org

Hawaii
Phone: 1-808-591-9772
Fax: 1-808-591-9776
Email: hi@happy-science.org
Website: happyscience-usa.org

Kauai
3343 Kanakolu Street, Suite 5
Lihue, HI 96766, USA
Phone: 1-808-822-7007
Fax: 1-808-822-6007
Email: kauai-hi@happy-science.org
Website: happyscience-usa.org

Toronto
845 The Queensway Etobicoke,
ON M8Z 1N6, Canada
Phone: 1-416-901-3747
Email: toronto@happy-science.org
Website: happy-science.ca

Vancouver
#201-2607 East 49th Avenue,
Vancouver, BC, V5S 1J9, Canada
Phone: 1-604-437-7735
Fax: 1-604-437-7764
Email: vancouver@happy-science.org
Website: happy-science.ca

INTERNATIONAL

Tokyo
1-6-7 Togoshi, Shinagawa,
Tokyo, 142-0041, Japan
Phone: 81-3-6384-5770
Fax: 81-3-6384-5776
Email: tokyo@happy-science.org
Website: happy-science.org

Seoul
74, Sadang-ro 27-gil, Dongjak-gu,
Seoul, Korea
Phone: 82-2-3478-8777
Fax: 82-2-3478-9777
Email: korea@happy-science.org
Website: happyscience-korea.org

London
3 Margaret St.London,
W1W 8RE United Kingdom
Phone: 44-20-7323-9255
Fax: 44-20-7323-9344
Email: eu@happy-science.org
Website: www.happyscience-uk.org

Taipei
No. 89, Lane 155, Dunhua N. Road,
Songshan District, Taipei City 105, Taiwan
Phone: 886-2-2719-9377
Fax: 886-2-2719-5570
Email: taiwan@happy-science.org
Website: happyscience-tw.org

Sydney
516 Pacific Highway, Lane Cove North,
2066 NSW, Australia
Phone: 61-2-9411-2877
Fax: 61-2-9411-2822
Email: sydney@happy-science.org

Kuala Lumpur
No 22A, Block 2, Jalil Link Jalan Jalil
Jaya 2, Bukit Jalil 57000,
Kuala Lumpur, Malaysia
Phone: 60-3-8998-7877
Fax: 60-3-8998-7977
Email: malaysia@happy-science.org
Website: happyscience.org.my

Sao Paulo
Rua. Domingos de Morais 1154,
Vila Mariana, Sao Paulo SP
CEP 04010-100, Brazil
Phone: 55-11-5088-3800
Email: sp@happy-science.org
Website: happyscience.com.br

Kathmandu
Kathmandu Metropolitan City,
Ward No. 15, Ring Road, Kimdol,
Sitapaila Kathmandu, Nepal
Phone: 977-1-427-2931
Email: nepal@happy-science.org

Jundiai
Rua Congo, 447, Jd. Bonfiglioli
Jundiai-CEP, 13207-340, Brazil
Phone: 55-11-4587-5952
Email: jundiai@happy-science.org

Kampala
Plot 877 Rubaga Road, Kampala
P.O. Box 34130 Kampala, UGANDA
Phone: 256-79-4682-121
Email: uganda@happy-science.org

ABOUT IRH PRESS

IRH Press Co., Ltd., based in Tokyo, was founded in 1987 as a publishing division of Happy Science. IRH Press publishes religious and spiritual books, journals, magazines and also operates broadcast and film production enterprises. For more information, visit *okawabooks.com*.

Follow us on:

Facebook: Okawa Books
Goodreads: Ryuho Okawa
Pinterest: Okawa Books

Twitter: Okawa Books
Instagram: OkawaBooks

─────── **NEWSLETTER** ───────

To receive book related news, promotions and events, please subscribe to our newsletter below.

✆ eepurl.com/bsMeJj

─────── **OKAWA BOOK CLUB PODCAST** ───────

A conversation about Ryuho Okawa's titles, topics ranging from self-help, current affairs, spirituality and religions. Available at iTunes, Spotify and Amazon Music.

BOOKS BY RYUHO OKAWA

RYUHO OKAWA'S LAWS SERIES

The Laws Series is an annual volume of books that are mainly comprised of Ryuho Okawa's lectures that function as universal guidance to all people. They are of various topics that were given in accordance with the changes that each year brings. *The Laws of the Sun*, the first publication of the laws series, ranked in the annual best-selling list in Japan in 1994. Since, the laws series' titles have ranked in the annual best-selling list every year for more than two decades, setting socio-cultural trends in Japan and around the world.

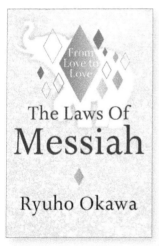

The *28th* Laws Series
The Laws Of Messiah

From Love to Love

Paperback • 248 pages • $16.95
ISBN: 978-1-942125-90-7

"What is Messiah?" This book carries an important message of love and guidance to people living now from the Modern-Day Messiah or the Modern-Day Savior. It also reveals the secret of Shambhala, the spiritual center of Earth, as well as the truth that this spiritual center is currently in danger of perishing and what we can do to protect this sacred place.

Love your Lord God. Know that those who don't know love don't know God. Discover the true love of God and the ideal practice of faith. This book teaches the most important element we must not lose sight of as we go through our soul training on Earth.

For a complete list of books, visit okawabooks.com

THE TRILOGY

The first three volumes of the Laws Series, *The Laws of the Sun*, *The Golden Laws*, and *The Nine Dimensions* make a trilogy that completes the basic framework of the teachings of God's Truths. *The Laws of the Sun* discusses the structure of God's Laws, *The Golden Laws* expounds on the doctrine of time, and *The Nine Dimensions* reveals the nature of space.

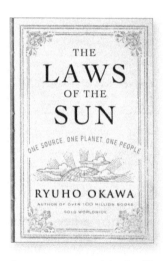

THE LAWS OF THE SUN

ONE SOURCE, ONE PLANET, ONE PEOPLE

Paperback • 288 pages • $15.95
ISBN: 978-1-942125-43-3

IMAGINE IF YOU COULD ASK GOD why He created this world and what spiritual laws He used to shape us—and everything around us. If we could understand His designs and intentions, we could discover what our goals in life should be and whether our actions move us closer to those goals or farther away.

At a young age, a spiritual calling prompted Ryuho Okawa to outline what he innately understood to be universal truths for all humankind. In *The Laws of the Sun*, Okawa outlines these laws of the universe and provides a road map for living one's life with greater purpose and meaning.

In this powerful book, Ryuho Okawa reveals the transcendent nature of consciousness and the secrets of our multidimensional universe and our place in it. By understanding the different stages of love and following the Buddhist Eightfold Path, he believes we can speed up our eternal process of development. *The Laws of the Sun* shows the way to realize true happiness—a happiness that continues from this world through the other.

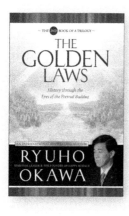

THE GOLDEN LAWS
HISTORY THROUGH THE EYES OF THE ETERNAL BUDDHA

Paperback • 201 pages • $14.95
ISBN: 978-1-941779-81-1

Throughout history, Great Guiding Spirits have been present on Earth in both the East and the West at crucial points in human history to further our spiritual development. *The Golden Laws* reveals how Divine Plan has been unfolding on Earth, and outlines 5,000 years of the secret history of humankind. Once we understand the true course of history, through past, present and into the future, we cannot help but become aware of the significance of our spiritual mission in the present age.

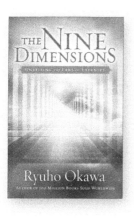

THE NINE DIMENSIONS
UNVEILING THE LAWS OF ETERNITY

Paperback • 168 pages • $15.95
ISBN: 978-0-982698-56-3

This book is a window into the mind of our loving God, who designed this world and the vast, wondrous world of our afterlife as a school with many levels through which our souls learn and grow. When the religions and cultures of the world discover the truth of their common spiritual origin, they will be inspired to accept their differences, come together under faith in God, and build an era of harmony and peaceful progress on Earth.

For a complete list of books, visit okawabooks.com

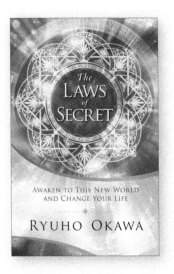

THE LAWS OF SECRET

AWAKEN TO THIS NEW WORLD
AND CHANGE YOUR LIFE

Paperback • 248 pages • $16.95
ISBN:978-1-942125-81-5

Our physical world coexists with the multi-dimensional spirit world and we are constantly interacting with some kind of spiritual energy, whether positive or negative, without consciously realizing it. This book reveals how our lives are affected by invisible influences, including the spiritual reasons behind influenza, the novel coronavirus infection, and other illnesses. The new view of the world in this book will inspire you to change your life in a better direction, and to become someone who can give hope and courage to others in this age of confusion.

For a complete list of books, visit okawabooks.com

THE TEN PRINCIPLES
FROM EL CANTARE VOLUME I

RYUHO OKAWA'S FIRST LECTURES
ON HIS BASIC TEACHINGS

Paperback • 232 pages • $16.95
ISBN: 978-1-942125-85-3

This book contains the historic lectures given on the first
five principles of the Ten Principles of Happy Science from
the author, Ryuho Okawa, who is revered as World Teacher.
These lectures produced an enthusiastic fellowship in
Happy Science Japan and became the foundation of the
current global utopian movement. You can learn the essence
of Okawa's teachings and the secret behind the rapid growth
of the Happy Science movement in simple language.

For a complete list of books, visit okawabooks.com

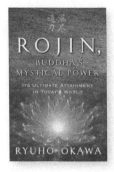

ROJIN, BUDDHA'S MYSTICAL POWER

ITS ULTIMATE ATTAINMENT IN TODAY'S WORLD

Paperback • 232 pages • $16.95
ISBN: 978-1-942125-82-2

In this book, Ryuho Okawa has redefined the traditional Buddhist term *Rojin* and explained that in modern society it means the following: the ability for individuals with great spiritual powers to live in the world as people with common sense while using their abilities to the optimal level. This book will unravel the mystery of the mind and lead you to the path to enlightenment.

THE POWER OF BASICS

INTRODUCTION TO MODERN ZEN LIFE OF CALM, SPIRITUALITY AND SUCCESS

Paperback • 232 pages • $16.95
ISBN:978-1-942125-75-4

The power of basics is a necessary asset to excel at any kind of work. It is the power to meticulously pursue tasks with a quiet Zen mindset. If you master this power of basics, you can achieve new levels of productivity regardless of your profession, and attain new heights of success and happiness. This book also describes the essence of an intellectual life, thereby reviving the true spirit of Zen in the modern age.

THE STRONG MIND

THE ART OF BUILDING THE INNER STRENGTH TO OVERCOME LIFE'S DIFFICULTIES

Paperback • 192 pages • $15.95
ISBN: 978-1-942125-36-5

The strong mind is what we need to rise time and again, and to move forward no matter what difficulties we face in life. This book will inspire and empower you to take courage, develop a mature and cultivated heart, and achieve resilience and hardiness so that you can break through the barriers of your limits and keep winning in the battle of your life.

For a complete list of books, visit <u>okawabooks.com</u>

SPIRITUAL MESSAGES FROM YAIDRON

SAVE THE WORLD FROM DESTRUCTION

Paperback • 190 pages • $11.95
ISBN: 978-1-943928-23-1

In this book, Yaidron explains what was going on behind the military coup in Myanmar and Taliban's control over Afghanistan. He also warns of the imminent danger approaching Taiwan. According to what he observes from the universe, World War III has already begun on Earth. What is now going on is a battle between democratic values and the communist one-party control. How to overcome this battle and create peace on Earth depends on the faith and righteous actions of each one of us.

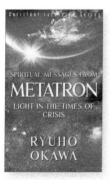

SPIRITUAL MESSAGES FROM METATRON

LIGHT IN THE TIMES OF CRISIS

Paperback • 146 pages • $11.95
ISBN: 978-1-943928-19-4

Metatron is one of the highest-ranking angels (seraphim) in Judaism and Christianity, and also one of the saviors of universe who has guided the civilizations of many planets including Earth, under the guidance of Lord God. Such savior has sent a message upon seeing the crisis of Earth. You will also learn about the truth behind the coronavirus pandemic, the unimaginable extent of China's desire, the danger of appeasement policy toward China, and the secret of Metatron.

ALIEN INVASION

CAN WE DEFEND EARTH?

Paperback • 190 pages • $9.95
ISBN: 978-1-941779-57-6

Why did Professor Hawking start to warn the threat of aliens? Who is giving spiritual guidance to Professor Hawking? How can we tell the difference between good aliens and bad aliens? This book reveals alien's plan to invade the Earth and how to counter them.

For a complete list of books, visit okawabooks.com

THE DESCENT OF ELOHIM
Spiritual Messages for the Movie,
The Laws of the Universe - The Age of Elohim

THE LAWS OF FAITH
One World Beyond Differences

THE LAWS OF MISSION
Essential Truths for Spiritual Awakening in a Secular Age

TWICEBORN
My Early Thoughts that Revealed My True Mission

JOHN LENNON'S MESSAGE FROM HEAVEN
On the Spirit of Love and Peace, Music,
and the Incredible Secret of His Soul

UFOS CAUGHT ON CAMERA!
A Spiritual Investigation on Videos and Photos
of the Luminous Objects Visiting Earth

SPIRITUAL MESSAGES FROM
THE GUARDIAN SPIRIT OF STAN LEE
Advice for *The Laws of the Universe - The Age of Elohim*

WITH SAVIOR
Messages from Space Being Yaidron

THE TRUTH ABOUT WWII
Justice Pal Speaks on the Tokyo Trials

For a complete list of books, visit okawabooks.com

MUSIC BY RYUHO OKAWA

El Cantare Ryuho Okawa Original Songs

A song celebrating Lord God

A song celebrating Lord God,
the God of the Earth,
who is beyond a prophet.

DVD
CD

The Water Revolution

English and Chinese version

For the truth and happiness of the 1.4 billion people in China who have no freedom. Love, justice, and sacred rage of God are on this melody that will give you courage to fight to bring peace.

DVD

CD

Search on YouTube

the water revolution for a short ad!

Listen now today!

 Download from
Spotify iTunes Amazon

DVD, CD available at amazon.com, and Happy Science locations worldwide

With Savior *English version*

This is the message of hope to the modern people who are living in the midst of the Coronavirus pandemic, natural disasters, economic depression, and other various crises.

Search on YouTube

with savior   for a short ad!

The Thunder

a composition for repelling the Coronavirus

We have been granted this music from our Lord. It will repel away the novel Coronavirus originated in China. Experience this magnificent powerful music.

Search on YouTube

the thunder coronavirus

for a short ad!

The Exorcism

prayer music for repelling Lost Spirits

Feel the divine vibrations of this Japanese and Western exorcising symphony to banish all evil possessions you suffer from and to purify your space!

Search on YouTube

the exorcism repelling

for a short ad!

Lightning Source UK Ltd.
Milton Keynes UK
UKHW010647100622
404239UK00001B/139